Apocalypse Codes

Decoding the Prophecies in the Book of Daniel

by Robert Rite

Table of Contents

Get Complimentary Access to: "Prophecy Alerts"

Dear Reader: Prophecies are being fulfilled so rapidly in these last days that I am offering my readers complimentary access to "*prophecy alerts*" so that you get "*Breaking Prophecy News*" as soon as it breaks…Just follow this link below and sign Up today…
http://robertritebooks.com/prophecy-alerts/

Chapter 1 - Daniel, an Example of how Faithfulness Unlocks Supernatural Blessings

As you will discover upon reading this book, the book of Daniel is probably the most important prophecy book in the Old Testament. An important point to recognize is that the visions and prophecies that Daniel received were all from God, through His messenger, the Archangel Gabriel.

Keep in mind that chapter one of Daniel, is just a warm-up for the many incredible prophecies that will be revealed in subsequent chapters. Here is a summary of some of the prophecies and mysteries that will be unlocked for you in this book:

- America in Prophecy, Babylon the Great, the 666, Antichrist, and More!
- King Nebuchadnezzar's dream of the "large image with the head of Gold, and feet of bronze mixed with clay".
- The "miracle in the Fiery Furnace".
- King Nebuchadnezzar's dream of the "collapse of the giant tree"
- The interpretation of the "Finger writing on the wall"
- The meaning behind "Daniel in the Lion's Den"
- Daniel's Dream of the "Four Great Beasts"
- Daniel's vision of the Ram and Goat
- Daniel's "seventy Weeks" prophecy
- Vision of the "Glorious man dressed in Linen"
- Interpretation of the Kings of North and South
- Prophecies for the End of Days - Apocalypse

As we will see, Daniel the Prophet of God should be also studied as an example of how we should all live our lives. He is one of very few patriarchs of the bible in whom no sin was ever recorded.

The whole purpose of this book is to unlock the secret meanings for you of the many prophecies in the book of Daniel for these last days!

You will also learn how natural man is not evolving, as this fallen world wants you to believe. He is mutating into what Satan wants him to become - a **beast** before the eyes of God.

So what we will do is read key passages and prophecies from the book of Daniel and then I will explain what they mean. Let's begin:

Daniel 1:1

"In the third year of the reign of Jehoiakim king of Judah, Nebuchadnezzar king of Babylon came to Jerusalem and besieged it."

The stage is set with Daniel and many of his Hebrew peoples being held captive in Babylon. Of all the captives, the book focuses on only four. A captive Jew in Babylon, Daniel and 3 other young men were required to serve a very proud king who like Pharaoh of Egypt in Moses time, did not know the God of the Hebrews.

The Babylonians served many gods of which Bel was their main god. But as we will discover, God who rules over all the kingdoms of the earth would use this King as well to fulfill and disclose many end time prophecies despite Daniel's exile!

The word **Babylon itself means confusion** and it was born out of mankind's lusts of the flesh and sin - and this applies to the world throughout this age and mankind at the end of the age. As you will learn this Babylon which symbolizes man's government continues to grow in confusion and corruption, until in the end of days (apocalypse) it is referred to as **"Babylon the Great"** (**Revelation 17**). More on this later.

God allowed this Jewish exile due to their reluctance to worship and serve only Him. Like their neighbors in Babylon, and like many today, they wanted to serve many Gods thus violating the first and most important commandment.

The name Daniel in Hebrew means God is Judge, yet the names of the other three young men who accompanied Daniel all had meanings of God's goodness"! But just like God has a special name for all of us the prince of this world wants to change our name to represent the devil - and claim our soul as his own! Let's read the first key passage:

Daniel 1:3-6

3 "Then the king instructed Ashpenaz, the master of his eunuchs, to bring some of the children of Israel and some of the king's descendants and some of the nobles,
4 young men in whom there was no blemish, but good-looking, gifted in all wisdom, possessing knowledge and quick to understand, who had ability to serve in the king's palace, and whom they might teach the language and literature of the Chaldeans.
5 And the king appointed for them a daily provision of the king's delicacies and of the wine which he drank, and three years of training for them, so that at the end of that time they might serve before the king.
*6 now **from among those of the sons of Judah were Daniel,***

Just like He does with all his faithful servants God made sure that even in captivity His people excel. And as we read in the passage above, the king called for the best of the exiled, to be as noble free men and not as slaves, to serve in his chamber. Among these would be Daniel and three other Hebrew lads. A hidden message here is that similarly God calls us out from the slavery of sin that we may be free and noble in God's eyes.

They would be under the guide of a Chaldean teacher (a spiritualist, magicians, astrologer, sorcerers, occult practitioners, magi types considered to be among the wisest in those days), and would be allowed to partake in the kings menu of wine and meat and other choice delicacies.

Daniel 1:6-7

"Now from among those of the sons of Judah was Daniel, Hananiah, Mishael, and Azariah. To them the chief of the eunuchs gave names: he gave Daniel the name Belteshazzar; to Hananiah, Shadrach; to Mishael, Meshach; and to Azariah, Abednego."

So the Prince assigned different names of these four special lads as follows:

Daniel's name was changed to Belteshazzar
Hananiah's name was changed to Shadrach
Mishael's name was changed to Meshach
Azariah's name was changed to - Abednago
Daniel's name means "***God is Judge***", and it was changed to Belteshazzar which means "***Bel preserves***".

So for all four lads, the names were changed from representing the goodness of God, to representing the perceived goodness of their pagan gods! Oh how cunning and vindictive is the prince of darkness! And this is just the first of the many truths that will be revealed in this great book of Daniel!

As we read throughout the book of Daniel we note however that they continue to be referred to by their Hebrew names - inferring that God always knows us by our real name, and He continues to love us, even when we separate ourselves from him because of our transgressions and sins. When we repent and return to him, he is right there willing to take us back.

God had spoken through the prophet Jeremiah just before the Jewish exile into Babylon, which occurred because not one righteous man was found in Israel - and of course not one righteous man can be found in this world, thus we are all dependent on the blood of the Lamb of God, for our Salvation.

Daniel 1:8

"But Daniel purposed in his heart that he would not defile himself with the portion of the king's delicacies, nor with the wine which he drank; therefore he requested of the chief of the eunuchs that he might not defile himself."

The king would also allow them to partake of his best wine and choice foods - which was an honor that one could not refuse. But Daniel refused to defile himself and instead courageously negotiated a different menu and managed to convince the prince in charge (through the grace of God I am sure) to allow them to eat only clean foods (vegetables and water instead of choice meats and wine). Symbolically he was choosing chastity over the pleasures of life. And as we read below, the steward consented even at risk of death for disobeying the king's order!

Daniel 1:9-14

9 "Now God had brought Daniel into the favor and goodwill of the chief of the eunuchs.

10 And the chief of the eunuchs said to Daniel, "I fear my lord the king, who has appointed your food and drink. For why should he see your faces looking worse than the young men who are your age? Then you would endanger my head before the king.

11 So Daniel said to the steward whom the chief of the eunuchs had set over Daniel, Hananiah, Mishael, and Azariah,

12 Please test your servants for ten days, and let them give us vegetables to eat and water to drink.

13 Then let our appearance be examined before you, and the appearance of the young men who eat the portion of the king's delicacies; and as you see fit, so deal with your servants."

14 So he consented with them in this matter, and tested them ten days."

15 And at the end of ten days their features appeared better and fatter in flesh than all the young men who ate the portion of the king's delicacies.

16 Thus the steward took away their portion of delicacies and the wine that they were to drink, and gave them vegetables."

As we see in Daniel 1:15 and 16 above, at the end of ten days the Hebrews that were fed just the vegetables looked better than those who ate the kings "delicacies"! So here is a recipe straight from heaven given over 2500 years ago for those who want to stay healthy - **eat vegetables**! And through the grace of God, they were excused from having to eat the king's unclean food.

Daniel 1:17

"As for these four young men, God gave them knowledge and skill in all literature and wisdom; and Daniel had understanding in all visions and dreams."

Daniel 1:17-21

17 "As for these four young men, God gave them knowledge and skill in all literature and wisdom; and Daniel had understanding in all visions and dreams.
18 Now at the end of the days, when the king had said that they should be brought in, the chief of the eunuchs brought them in before Nebuchadnezzar.
19 Then the king interviewed them, and among them all none was found like Daniel, Hananiah, Mishael, and Azariah; therefore they served before the king.
20 And in all matters of wisdom and understanding about which the king examined them, he found them ten times better than all the magicians and astrologers who were in all his realm.
21 Thus Daniel continued until the first year of King Cyrus."

For their courage and obedience, in not defiling themselves by eating unclean food, God blessed these four men with wisdom and intelligence so that they could excel over the others in the sciences and teachings of the time.

Daniel also received a special blessing of prophecy through visions and dreams - and in the later case his teacher would be the Archangel of the Lord! The King soon noticed these Lads as very special and found them ten times "better" than his choice magicians and astrologers:

The message behind Daniel chapter 1

We can indeed serve God, instead of the gods of this world, and resist all worldly temptations of the flesh, despite seemingly insurmountable odds and for our loyalty, God will bless us exponentially and beyond

11

what one can imagine. This truth is brought home as well in the following verse:

Daniel 12:10
"Many shall be purified, made white, and refined, but the wicked shall do wickedly; and none of the wicked shall understand, but the wise shall understand."

Because of his steadfast faith and loyalty, God greatly favored Daniel. So much so that when Daniel asked for an explanation, God answered and even sent Gabriel to reveal and explain Daniel's dreams and visions to him. In fact Michael, one of God's chief Archangels, spent twenty-one days fighting along-side Gabriel, just so that Daniel's prayers could be answered that he could receive the prophecies related to his visions. Likewise, Gabriel said that from the moment that Daniel opened his heart to understand, the response came. So much regarded was Daniel that he would be receiving the prophecies related to the very time of the end in the last six chapters of the book (Daniel 12:4, and 12:13)

Daniel 12:13

"But you, go your way till the end; for you shall rest, and will arise to your inheritance at the end of the days."

Chapter 2 - King Nebuchadnezzar's Dream of the Large Image

In chapter 2 of Daniel - the king had a dream and he requests his Chaldeans, magicians and astrologers to interpret it even though the king could not remember the dream! How's that for an impossible assignment! Let's read part of the passages:

Daniel 2:5-6; 10

5 *"The king answered and said to the Chaldeans, "My decision is firm: if you do not make known the dream to me, and its interpretation, you shall be cut in pieces, and your houses shall be made an ash heap.*
6 However, if you tell the dream and its interpretation, you shall receive from me gifts, rewards, and great honor. Therefore tell me the dream and its interpretation."
10 "The Chaldeans answered the king, and said, "There is not a man on earth who can tell the king's matter; therefore no king, lord, or ruler has ever asked such things of any magician, astrologer, or Chaldean.
11 It is a difficult thing that the king requests, and there is no other who can tell it to the king except the gods, whose dwelling is not with flesh."

As usual, none of the Chaldeans could interpret the king's dream. None except God's elect - of course! Now the king issued a decree that all the wise men of Babylon be killed for their inability to perform one of their primary jobs, that of interpreting the king's dream. Let's take it up at verse 2:24

Daniel 2:24

*"Therefore Daniel went to Arioch, whom the king had appointed to destroy the wise men of Babylon. He went and said thus to him: "**Do not destroy the wise men of Babylon**; take me before the king, and I will tell the king the interpretation."*

So we see Daniel being a symbol of and **playing the role of Jesus** here, as he intercedes for the Chaldeans (symbolic of sin). Like Jesus, Daniel did not judge those sinners, rather he asked the king for time so that he can interpret the dream. Thus the Chaldean's lives are all spared.

Daniel 2:27-30

27 Daniel answered in the presence of the king, and said, "The secret which the king has demanded, the wise men, the astrologers, the magicians, and the soothsayers cannot declare to the king.
28 but there is a God in heaven who reveals secrets, and He has made known to King Nebuchadnezzar what will be in the latter days. Your dream, and the visions of your head upon your bed, were these:
29 As for you, O king, thoughts came to your mind while on your bed, about what would come to pass after this; and He who reveals secrets has made known to you what will be.
30 but as for me, this secret has not been revealed to me because I have more wisdom than anyone living, but for our sakes who make known the interpretation to the king, and that you may know the thoughts of your heart."

From the above we see that before Daniel interprets the king's dream, he gives full credit and glory to God. Then he proceeds to interpret the dream as follows:

Daniel 2:31-45:

31 "You, O king, were watching; and behold, a great image! This great image, whose splendor was excellent, stood before you; and its form was awesome."
32 "This image's head was of fine gold, its chest and arms of silver, its belly and thighs[a] of bronze,
33 its legs of iron, its feet partly of iron and partly of clay.
34 You watched while a stone was cut out without hands, which struck the image on its feet of iron and clay, and broke them in pieces.
35 Then the iron, the clay, the bronze, the silver, and the gold

15

were crushed together, and became like chaff from the summer threshing floors; the wind carried them away so that no trace of them was found. And the stone that struck the image became a great mountain and filled the whole earth.

36 This is the dream. Now we will tell the interpretation of it before the king.

37 You, O king, are a king of kings. For the God of heaven has given you a kingdom, power, strength, and glory;

38 and wherever the children of men dwell, or the beasts of the field and the birds of the heaven, He has given them into your hand, and has made you ruler over them all—you are this head of gold.

39 but after you shall arise another kingdom inferior to yours; then another, a third kingdom of bronze, which shall rule over all the earth.

40 And the fourth kingdom shall be as strong as iron, inasmuch as iron breaks in pieces and shatters everything; and like iron that crushes, that kingdom will break in pieces and crush all the others.

41 Whereas you saw the feet and toes, partly of potter's clay and partly of iron, the kingdom shall be divided; yet the strength of the iron shall be in it, just as you saw the iron mixed with ceramic clay.

42 And as the toes of the feet were partly of iron and partly of clay, so the kingdom shall be partly strong and partly fragile.

43 As you saw iron mixed with ceramic clay, they will mingle with the seed of men; but they will not adhere to one another, just as iron does not mix with clay.

44 And in the days of these kings the God of heaven will set up a kingdom which shall never be destroyed; and the kingdom shall not be left to other people; it shall break in pieces and consume all these kingdoms, and it shall stand forever.

45 Inasmuch as you saw that the stone was cut out of the mountain without hands, and that it broke in pieces the iron, the bronze, the clay, the silver, and the gold—the great God has made known to the king what will come to pass after this. The dream is certain, and its interpretation is sure."

The key point behind this image is that this very large image starts out with a head made of gold, and gradually deteriorates from a Golden head to feet of iron mixed with clay - a very unstable foundation, wouldn't you say!

This image is clearly depicting how all the kingdoms of earth through time have continued to decay, degrade and become corrupted as they are mingled with the clay of paganism, injustice, unrighteousness, sin, and blasphemy against the only true God. Today we are living in the unstable feet or iron mixed (weakened) with clay. Eventually they all collapse, and this degenerate **"Babylon" style world** that has existed throughout this age, will give way to a coming glorious kingdom that will last forever.

We see that this image of nations beginning with ancient Babylon starts out in great shape unified and solid gold - perhaps even with some of God's blessings it prospered and had no rival at its peak. But the future kingdoms that would emerge would gradually deteriorate in strength, unity and effectiveness. At the bottom of the image (symbolic with the end of this age) we see that the final kingdom will be composed of steel mixed with clay - hardly stable and vulnerable to collapse the entire image (end this entire age). The king actually welcomed this dream because Daniel told him that his kingdom was the head of Gold. He obviously did not understand that his kingdom, being part of the entire image would also collapse.

In Dan. 2:37 Interesting that Daniel refers to him as the king here as **a king of kings** (**not *the King of Kings***). He is referring to the king as a replica or better yet an imposter of the coming King of Kings. This king of Babylon symbolizes all the future kings of this earth that would follow him. The dream is succinctly declaring that his Babylonian style kingdom (full of enduring pagan worship throughout our entire age), will endure until the very end of this age, when then Satan and his Babylonian system will finally be brought down and crushed (**Rev. 18:21**) just like the giant image in the king's dream. It will crushed by the Lion of the Tribe of Judah - "**the true**" King of Kings.

In **Daniel 2:44** it is made clear that this Babylonian style kingdom will eventually be replaced with God's kingdom which will endure forever:

Daniel 2:44

" And in the days of these kings the God of heaven will set up a kingdom which shall never be destroyed; and the kingdom shall not be left to other people; it shall break in pieces and consume all these kingdoms, and it shall stand forever."

During the time of this dream, the system of Babylon operated under just one king, a ruthless king at that. This is just like in the last days in which the world will be temporarily under the control of an evil world ruler - and interestingly his kingdom will be called Babylon, but because of its size and power it is referred to as "Babylon the Great" (**Revelation 18**). And it too will be totally destroyed:

Revelation 18:21

"Then a mighty angel took up a stone like a great millstone and threw it into the sea, saying, Thus with violence the great city Babylon shall be thrown down, and shall not be found anymore."

At the end of Daniel's interpretation (**Dan. 2:46**) **_the king fell on his face, and humbled himself before Daniel._** Daniel, Just like Joseph in Egypt was relegated to second in command. This is symbolic of when Jesus returns and all peoples, nations, and kings will bow down before him (every knee shall bow before the Lamb).

Romans 14:11

"For it is written: "*As* I live, says the Lord, **Every knee shall bow** to Me, and **every** tongue **shall** confess to God."

Daniel 2:49

"Also Daniel petitioned the king, and he set Shadrach, Meshach, and Abednego over the affairs of the province of Babylon; but Daniel *sat* in the gate of the king."

In **Daniel 2:49** we see how Daniel petitioned the king to assign positions of nobility to the other 3 Hebrew friends - just like Jesus petitions God to assign his elect to positions of nobility in paradise as kings and priests, wearing white robes and crowns of Gold!

Revelation 5:10
"And have made us kings and priests to our God; and we shall reign on the earth."

Note: As you have and will continue to see, it is interesting to witness how these pagan kings all recognize and even refer to our Lord as the "Most high", and even as the "Most Holy", yet, just like fallen man, they refuse to worship or surrender to the true God! Not even after they witnessed great miracles.

This lack of reverence to the sovereign God persists perhaps even more today where not only the nations, but also the peoples refuse to acknowledge that the bible is the word of God despite the fact that every bible prophecy has been fulfilled to date!

Chapter 3 - The "miracle in the Fiery Furnace"

Despite the dream that should have humbled king Nebuchadnezzar, instead he decides to erect this huge image (approximately 100 feet tall) of his gods, made of pure gold. And then he requires all to worship the image, at the peril of death. Let's read these verses.

Daniel 3:1-6

1 "Nebuchadnezzar the king made an image of gold, whose height was sixty cubits and its width six cubits. He set it up in the plain of Dura, in the province of Babylon.
2 And King Nebuchadnezzar sent word to gather together the satraps, the administrators, the governors, the counselors, the treasurers, the judges, the magistrates, and all the officials of the provinces, to come to the dedication of the image which King Nebuchadnezzar had set up.
3 So the satraps, the administrators, the governors, the counselors, the treasurers, the judges, the magistrates, and all the officials of the provinces gathered together for the dedication of the image that King Nebuchadnezzar had set up; and they stood before the image that Nebuchadnezzar had set up.
4 Then a herald cried aloud: "To you it is commanded, O peoples, nations, and languages,
5 that at the time you hear the sound of the horn, flute, harp, lyre, and psaltery, in symphony with all kinds of music, you shall fall down and worship the gold image that King Nebuchadnezzar has set up;
6 and whoever does not fall down and worship shall be cast immediately into the midst of a burning fiery furnace."

In **Revelation chapter 13,** we also read that the end time one world government leader and his false prophet, a symbol of the Chaldeans of Daniels time and their pagan gods of "***Babylon the great***", will also force mankind to worship the image of the beast:

Revelation 13:15

"He was granted power to give breath to the image of the beast, that the image of the beast should both speak and cause as many as would not worship the image of the beast to be killed."

The message behind this prophecy is clear - while in the time of Daniel those under the control of Babylon were required to worship the king's image, in the last days all mankind will be required to worship the beast's (Satan's) image!

Take note how the beast, Satan has grown from this small serpent on a tree (Genesis 3:1-7) to a massive beast in Revelation 13 now referred to as "Babylon the great". The food for the serpent has always been sin, and because iniquity has grown exponentially on earth, this is why the beast of Revelation has grown so massive (Rev. 12:3); his influence and reach is global.

The other meaning behind this golden image speaks of the mindset of the king (carnal man's nature). Although he already knew the fate of all kingdoms operating outside of the will of God, he tried to fix the problem all by himself by erecting the perfect kingdom - an image of his kingdom made of pure Gold. He forsook God's message and decided to erect his own image made of pure Gold from head to toe, without the imperfections of clay.

The message behind this story is that Like fallen man void of God, we try to fix all of our problems all by ourselves. Because of his arrogance and confused pagan mindset, he misinterpreted the message of the dream as meaning that he was the head of gold, and therefore why not make an image of pure gold, as if this way his kingdom would last forever. Since he did not revere God, he required everyone to worship his image, instead of God!

Anyone who would not worship the king's image would be thrown into a burning fiery furnace. They chose this form of execution because among the gods that they worshipped, they held great reverence to their "god of fire". The kings purpose was to unify all the nations under his control to worship only him and his kingdom - eerily just like what the end time beast will endeavor to do (Rev. 13:15)

Dan. 3:12 - When the 3 young Hebrew lads whom Daniel assigned positions of authority refused to worship the image, their accusers who were probably jealous of their positions of power to begin with, accused them before the king, who immediately condemned these Hebrews to death by hell-like fire. Let's read as the governors accuse the young lads:

Daniel 3:12-15

12 "There are certain Jews whom you have set over the affairs of the province of Babylon: Shadrach, Meshach, and Abednego; these men, O king, have not paid due regard to you. They do not serve your gods or worship the gold image which you have set up.
13 Then Nebuchadnezzar, in rage and fury, gave the command to bring Shadrach, Meshach, and Abednego. So they brought these men before the king.
14 Nebuchadnezzar spoke, saying to them, "Is it true, Shadrach, Meshach, and Abednego, that you do not serve my gods or worship the gold image which I have set up?
15 Now if you are ready at the time you hear the sound of the

*horn, flute, harp, lyre, and psaltery, in symphony with all kinds
of music, and you fall down and worship the image which I have
made, good! But if you do not worship, you shall be cast
immediately into the midst of a burning fiery furnace. And
who is the god who will deliver you from my hands?"*

The governors and rulers under the king were
watching the three Hebrew boys carefully to find how
they could convict them, because they were jealous of
their position and felt that since they were Hebrews
from the captivity of Judah, they did not deserve any
position of honor. So as soon as they witnessed that
these boys would not worship the gods or images of
Babylon, they immediately told the king.

We will probably run into the same situation during
the apocalypse whereby the beast kingdom will have
spies among its inhabitants who will snitch out anyone
that does not worship the image of the beast.

Let us read how the lads responded:

Daniel 3:17-18

*17 "If that is the case, our God whom we serve is able to deliver
us from the burning fiery furnace, and He will deliver us from
your hand, O king.
18 But if not, let it be known to you, O king, that we do not serve
your gods, nor will we worship the gold image which you have
set up."*

Even though confronted with possible death by fire,
these brave souls refused to worship the image and
proclaimed that their God would deliver them from the
hell fire. These young men were willing to die for
their God than worship a false god!

23

Then King Nebuchadnezzar who was a very arrogant and rage-full leader became very angry at their refusal to worship him:

Daniel 3:19-22

19 "Then Nebuchadnezzar was full of fury, and the expression on his face changed toward Shadrach, Meshach, and Abednego. He spoke and commanded that they heat the furnace seven times more than it was usually heated.
20 And he commanded certain mighty men of valor who were in his army to bind Shadrach, Meshach, and Abednego, and cast them into the burning fiery furnace.
21 Then these men were bound in their coats, their trousers, their turbans, and their other garments, and were cast into the midst of the burning fiery furnace.
22 Therefore, because the king's command was urgent, and the furnace was exceedingly hot, the flame of the fire killed those men who took up Shadrach, Meshach, and Abednego."

So they were cast into the hell fire and then...the king could not believe his eyes as he saw four men in the fire and the fourth "***was like the Son of God***"!

Daniel 3:23-26

23 And these three men, Shadrach, Meshach, and Abednego, fell down bound into the midst of the burning fiery furnace.
*24 Then King Nebuchadnezzar was astonished; and he rose in haste and spoke, saying to his counselors, **"Did we not cast three men bound into the midst of the fire?"***
They answered and said to the king, "True, O king."
25 "Look!" he answered, "I see four men loose, walking in the midst of the fire; and they are not hurt, and the form of the fourth is like the Son of God."
26 Then Nebuchadnezzar went near the mouth of the burning fiery furnace and spoke, saying, "Shadrach, Meshach, and Abednego, servants of the Most High God, come out, and come here."

They were covered so they could not burn, just like Jesus is our covering that keeps us out of the true hell fire, which is the **"Lake of Fire"** revealed in **Revelation 20:14.**

Just like the three lads came out of the fire fully clothed and unburned, God's people, who have incorruptible souls, are not subject to the effects of the hell fire. Only the corruptible souls are subject to the hell fire.

Daniel 3:27-30

27 "And the satraps, administrators, governors, and the king's counselors gathered together, and they saw these men on whose bodies the fire had no power; the hair of their head was not singed nor were their garments affected, and the smell of fire was not on them.
28 Nebuchadnezzar spoke, saying, "Blessed be the God of Shadrach, Meshach, and Abednego, who sent His Angel[a] and delivered His servants who trusted in Him, and they have frustrated the king's word, and yielded their bodies, that they should not serve nor worship any god except their own God!
29 Therefore I make a decree that any people, nation, or language which speaks anything amiss against the God of Shadrach, Meshach, and Abednego shall be cut in pieces, and their houses shall be made an ash heap; because there is no other God who can deliver like this."
30 Then the king promoted Shadrach, Meshach, and Abednego in the province of Babylon."

Because of their courage, and resolute faith in God, not only did they come out of the fiery furnace unscathed, but Nebuchadnezzar ended up praising God, and these three were even promoted to positions of higher authority in the king's empire. How is that for a wild day at work!

The message here is literal and also dual. In the last days most or all of us will be required to worship the beast, the coming one world ruler, if we do not worship his image - at the risk of martyrdom. Will we also follow the example of these young lads in our moment of testing?

Revelation 13:15

*"He was granted power to give breath to the image of the beast, that the image of the beast should both speak **and cause as many as would not worship the image of the beast to be killed**"*

Chapter 4 - King Nebuchadnezzar's dream of the "collapse of the giant tree"

King Nebuchadnezzar has another dream which frightened him, but this one he was able to remember.

Once again he first calls upon everyone but the man of God Daniel. Just like in modern times Governments, leaders, and most of mankind consult the men of the world before thinking of consulting with God's elect. And once again, like fallen man, he seeks an answer from everyone except God. So, after the magicians and Chaldeans failed to interpret his dream as usual, he remembered, and calls upon Daniel:

Daniel 4:7-8

7 "Then the magicians, the astrologers, the Chaldeans, and the soothsayers came in, and I told them the dream; but they did not make known to me its interpretation.
8 But at last Daniel came before me (his name is Belteshazzar, according to the name of my god; in him is the Spirit of the Holy God), and I told the dream before him, saying:
9 Belteshazzar, chief of the magicians, because I know that the Spirit of the Holy God is in you, and no secret troubles you, explain to me the visions of my dream that I have seen, and its interpretation.

The king describes his dream as follows:

Daniel 4:10-17

10 "These were the visions of my head while on my bed: I was looking, and behold, a tree in the midst of the earth, and its height was great.

11 The tree grew and became strong; its height reached to the heavens, and it could be seen to the ends of all the earth.
12 Its leaves were lovely, its fruit abundant, and in it was food for all.
The beasts of the field found shade under it, the birds of the heavens dwelt in its branches, and all flesh was fed from it.
13 I saw in the visions of my head while on my bed, and there was a watcher, a holy one, coming down from heaven. 14 He cried aloud and said thus:
'Chop down the tree and cut off its branches, strip off its leaves and scatter its fruit.
Let the beasts get out from under it, and the birds from its branches.
15 Nevertheless leave the stump and roots in the earth, bound with a band of iron and bronze,
In the tender grass of the field. Let it be wet with the dew of heaven, and let him graze with the beasts on the grass of the earth.
16 Let his heart be changed from that of a man, let him be given the heart of a beast, and let seven times[a] pass over him.
17 'This decision is by the decree of the watchers, and the sentence by the word of the holy ones, in order that the living may know that the Most High rules in the kingdom of men, Gives it to whomever He will, and sets over it the lowest of men."

This time the interpretation that Daniel had to give the king was certainly not noble unlike the interpretation of the first dream, so Daniel had to pause for a bit to gather his words; having a kind spirit and respectful of authority, he was careful of offending the king. Here is the main meaning of the king's dream:

Daniel 4:24-27

24 "this is the interpretation, O king, and this is the decree of the Most High, which has come upon my lord the king:

25 They shall drive you from men, your dwelling shall be with the beasts of the field, and they shall make you eat grass like oxen. They shall wet you with the dew of heaven, and seven times shall pass over you, till you know that the Most High rules in the kingdom of men, and gives it to whomever He chooses.

26 "And in as much as they gave the command to leave the stump and roots of the tree, your kingdom shall be assured to you, after you come to know that Heaven rules.

27 Therefore O king, let my advice be acceptable to you; break off your sins by being righteous, and your iniquities by showing mercy to the poor. Perhaps there may be a lengthening of your prosperity."

As we will now read the king refused to listen to Daniel's advice to humble himself before God, and instead he credited himself for the size of his kingdom and all the power that he had acquired for himself. He believed that only he was responsible for the magnitude of his kingdom. Within just one year the curse was bestowed upon the king because once again he failed to heed the words of the Lord. Let's read what happened:

Daniel 4:28-33

28 "All this came upon King Nebuchadnezzar.

29 At the end of the twelve months he was walking about the royal palace of Babylon.

30 The king spoke, saying, **"Is not this great Babylon, that I have built for a royal dwelling by my mighty power and for the honor of my majesty?"**

31 While the word was still in the king's mouth, a voice fell from heaven: "King Nebuchadnezzar, to you it is spoken: the kingdom has departed from you!

32 And they shall drive you from men, and **your dwelling shall**

be with the beasts of the field. They shall make you eat
grass like oxen; and seven times shall pass over you, until
you know that the Most High rules in the kingdom of men,
and gives it to whomever He chooses."

33 That very hour the word was fulfilled concerning
Nebuchadnezzar; he was driven from men and ate grass like
oxen; his body was wet with the dew of heaven till his hair had
grown like eagles' feathers and his nails like birds' claws.

Then after the seven year curse was up, and the king
finally got the message, he humbled himself before
the Lord and said:

34 "And at the end of the time I, Nebuchadnezzar, lifted my eyes
to heaven, and my understanding returned to me; and I blessed
the Most High and praised and honored Him who lives forever:
For His dominion is an everlasting dominion, and His
kingdom is from generation to generation.
35 All the inhabitants of the earth are reputed as nothing; he
does according to His will in the army of heaven and among the
inhabitants of the earth. No one can restrain His hand or say to
Him, "What have you done?"
36 At the same time my reason returned to me, and for the glory
of my kingdom, my honor and splendor returned to me. My
counselors and nobles resorted to me, I was restored to my
kingdom, and excellent majesty was added to me.
37 Now I, Nebuchadnezzar, praise and extol and honor the King
of heaven, all of whose works are truth, and His ways justice.
And those who walk in pride He is able to put down."

So eventually the king regained his senses and mental
capacity back and this time he "finally" repented
(Dan. 4:34-37)

The Message behind Daniel Chapter 4

We must learn to humble ourselves before the Lord,

and to thank Him for everything we have. Whether we believe in God or not - he is in control of our lives. Our life belongs to God, whether we like it or not!

And just like this king, all of us receive many warnings throughout our life to stay on the right path. Unfortunately, many continue to ignore the word, the Lord and the warnings until they face devastating consequences or even life ending situations as king Nebuchadnezzar had to endure because of his arrogance.

Because of God's tuff love for the arrogant, some of us need to be put on our knees, before we finally get the message, and king Nebuchadnezzar finally humbled himself before the Lord and his situation improved greatly.

Being a picture if Jesus, Daniel had great empathy for the king, even though the king had done so much evil against Israel and its people (he had destroyed the holy city and taken the Jews into captivity). Like Jesus knows, Daniel knew through the dream the dire future that awaited the king. But in his mercy, he offered the king advice on what he needed to do to prevent the punishment:

Daniel 4:27
"Therefore, O king, approve my counsel and redeem thy sins with righteousness and thine iniquities with mercies unto the poor: behold the medicine for thy sin."

Just as the dream warned, Nebuchadnezzar (representative of carnal, stubborn and arrogant mankind) went mad and lost all capacity to rule or even to live like a human - he was relegated to living in the field like a beast. This is symbolic of what could happen to anyone who ignores God's warnings. This is why God refers to the last kingdom on earth as a beast.

Any kingdom, nation, peoples, or tongue that refuses to worship and obey God are relegated to a beast in the eyes of God! Indeed, God considers anyone with a corrupted soul - a beast. More than any other time in history, there are many beasts roaming the streets today. These have no heart or conscience - such as the cold blooded killers, mass murderers, rapists, among others that we read or hear about constantly and at an accelerated pace. There is no better term to use for these animals, then a "beast", wouldn't you agree?

Chapter 5 - The interpretation of the "Finger writing on the wall"

Nebuchadnezzar appears to no longer reign and in his place is his son Belshazzar, whose name means "Bel preserves the king". Just like the warnings of Nebuchadnezzar's first dream regarding the deterioration of subsequent kingdoms, his son's kingdom ends much quicker than his father's. While hosting a large banquet feast he decides to desecrate the Holy vessels that were taken from the Temple of Jerusalem, and instantly his fate was sealed. Let's read:

Dan. 5:3-4

"Then they brought the gold vessels that had been taken from the temple of the house of God which had been in Jerusalem; and the king and his lords, his wives, and his concubines drank from them. They drank wine, and praised the gods of gold and silver, bronze and iron, wood and stone."

He immediately saw handwriting on the wall. Just like his father before him, he first calls upon those he trusts (believes in) the most, his Chaldeans and magicians to interpret the meaning of the writing. And of course none of them could. Since they did not know God, they could never interpret God's dreams or visions - as they were spiritually blind! A spiritually blind soul can never speak, read or understand God's language!

The king, just like his predecessors, was confused and blinded just as the meaning behind the name of his kingdom (Babble), so that he trusted more in the gods of gold, silver and brass which cannot see, hear or know, than the God that knows everything.

Just like mortal man who first tries to resolve everything on their own merit without first seeking the Lord's guidance. As Jesus explained in **Mathew 6:23** - fallen man trusts in himself and other people (the darkness) more than the Lord (the lightness).

Today, like during ancient times, mankind places much more emphasis on the toys, gadgets and pleasures of the world (such as their computers, smart phones, social accounts and cars, etc.) rather than on the Lord who can secure eternal life. Where most of your time is invested or spent on, this is where your heart is. As the Lord said: We cannot serve both mammon (the pleasures, things and lusts of this world - including the god of money) and God:

Mathew 6:24

*"No one can serve two masters; for either he will hate the one and love the other, or else he will be loyal to the one and despise the other. You cannot serve God and **mammon**.*

The queen recommended Daniel to the king who being familiar with his spiritual power finally summoned him. And this is the interpretation that Daniel gave to the king:

Dan. 5:13-17

13 Then Daniel was brought in before the king. The king spoke, and said to Daniel, "Are you that Daniel who is one of the captives from Judah, whom my father the king brought from Judah?
14 I have heard of you, that the Spirit of God is in you, and that light and understanding and excellent wisdom are found in you.

15 Now the wise men, the astrologers, have been brought in before me, that they should read this writing and make known to me its interpretation, but they could not give the interpretation of the thing.
16 And I have heard of you, that you can give interpretations and explain enigmas. Now if you can read the writing and make known to me its interpretation, you shall be clothed with purple and have a chain of gold around your neck, and shall be the third ruler in the kingdom."
17 Then Daniel answered, and said before the king, "Let your gifts be for yourself, and give your rewards to another; yet I will read the writing to the king, and make known to him the interpretation."

The king offered Daniel great riches and honor if Daniel could interpret the meaning, but Daniel said he would interpret it without the reward and to give his reward to another. And why would he want a promotion from this king, since Daniel already knew that the king would be meeting his maker very shortly - that very night!

Daniel actually provides the king with even more information than the king probably wanted to hear. He begins to explain the reason for the message on the wall:

Daniel 5:18-24

18 "O king; the Most High God gave Nebuchadnezzar your father a kingdom and majesty, glory and honor.
19 And because of the majesty that He gave him, all peoples, nations, and languages trembled and feared before him. Whomever he wished, he executed; whomever he wished, he kept alive; whomever he wished, he set up; and whomever he wished, he put down.
20 But when his heart was lifted up, and his spirit was hardened in pride, he was deposed from his kingly throne, and they took his glory from him.

21 Then he was driven from the sons of men, his heart was made like the beasts, and his dwelling was with the wild donkeys. They fed him with grass like oxen, and his body was wet with the dew of heaven, till he knew that the Most High God rules in the kingdom of men, and appoints over it whomever He chooses.
22 "But you his son, Belshazzar, have not humbled your heart, although you knew all this.
23 And you have lifted yourself up against the Lord of heaven. They have brought the vessels of His house before you, and you and your lords, your wives and your concubines, have drunk wine from them. And you have praised the gods of silver and gold, bronze and iron, wood and stone, which do not see or hear or know; and the God who holds your breath in His hand and owns all your ways, you have not glorified.
24 Then the fingers of the hand were sent from Him, and this writing was written."

Notice how on verse 18 that Daniel reminds the king (and all of us) that God is the one that appoints us to any position of authority that we may enjoy in life **(Dan. 5:18),** and the arrogant and prideful person who refuses to acknowledge this truth, will usually pay a price. Besides, who needs a position of authority or great wealth in this temporary domain when the true and only award that matters awaits the faithful on the other side?

Now Daniel continues with the actual interpretation of the writing on the wall

Daniel 5:25:28

25 "And this is the inscription that was written:
MENE, MENE, TEKEL, UPHARSIN.
26 This is the interpretation of each word. MENE: God has

numbered your kingdom, and finished it;
27 TEKEL: You have been weighed in the balances, and found
wanting;
28 PERES: Your kingdom has been divided, and given to the
Medes and Persians."

That very night king Belshazzar **lost both his kingdom and his life**.

The Message Behind Daniel Chapter 5:

In the time of the end, there is another Babylon that will also fall in one hour as prophesied in the **book of Revelation**.

Revelation 18:9-10

" The kings of the earth who committed fornication and lived luxuriously with her will weep and lament for her, when they see the smoke of her burning, standing at a distance for fear of her torment, saying, 'Alas, alas, that great city Babylon, that mighty city! ***For in one hour your judgment has come.****'*

Folks, the level of the depravity of the world we live in today is no better and actually it is much GREATER than the condition of King Belshazzar and his kingdom. This is why in the last book of Revelation God refers to the religious (the people) and political (the nations) systems of the world just before the apocalypse as corrupted and thus worthy to wear the name of "**Babylon the Great**"

In Daniels time there were no bibles so that the only way people could receive the word of God was through divine inspiration, the prophets, judges and seers appointed by god - so that the king and the people in Daniels time erred many times due to their lack of knowledge.

But we today have **NO EXCUSE**. We have access to the word of God in many venues including the search engines, and online bibles, such as:
biblegateway.com - the latter of which I happen to Love, and it even offers all or most of the translations and versions!

In ancient days at least the people were more humble, in that they knew that they were not gods. In modern day Babylon, on the other hand, many think that God does not exist, or that they are gods.

Many today have forsaken and forgotten God, and His word. Many of these are the same folks that look up at the heavens and ask "why", as soon as any tragedy strikes.

When the Lord returns we will **_not_** be able to use the age-old excuse: "**but I did not know**". God even sent his only begotten Son Jesus Christ into the world approximately two thousand years ago to bear the cross of sin for all mankind - for anyone who would call upon His name and accept the gift of His blood for the redemption of our sins. Unlike the past and present gods of Babylon, the true God can see, hear and know!

Some may think that ignorance of the truth will exonerate them before the God of the universe; but it won't help in balancing the scales in their favor. For those who do not know Him, it's because they choose not to - but it is still not too late!

Chapter 6 - The meaning behind "Daniel in the Lion's Den"

Now the Kingdom of Babylon has fallen to the Medes of Persia. Since Daniel is under the favor of God, he has now outlasted 2 kings and the new king Darius, appointed Daniel as the first of his three presidents, even though he was appointed third under Belshazzar the night before Babylon fell. Boy did he move up the ranks quickly!

This of course led to jealousy among the other presidents and governors - and so they conspired to get rid of Daniel. Now unlike the Babylonians, the Medes placed the law above the king, and the presidents and governors would use this loophole in the law to try to destroy Daniel. So just like the first image, we see that this new king was less powerful than the Babylonian king as he was subject to the laws of the Medes. Yet, as we will soon see, Darius will be most instrumental in carrying out God's plans. Note how God uses the weak or the meek to carry on greatest tasks (i.e. Joseph, Moses, David, etc.).

They knew that Daniel would never obey a law that violated God's law. So in **Daniel 6:6-9** they trick the king into implementing a law that for thirty days no one can petition or pray to any God except to the king; the trusting king who not aware of their scheme agreed to this law.

Daniel 6:6-9

6 "So these governors and satraps thronged before the king, and

said thus to him: "King Darius, live forever!
7 All the governors of the kingdom, the administrators and
satraps, the counselors and advisors, have consulted together to
establish a royal statute and to make a firm decree, that
whoever petitions any god or man for thirty days, except
you, O king, shall be cast into the den of lions.
8 Now, O king, establish the decree and sign the writing, so that
it cannot be changed, according to the law of the Medes and
Persians, which does not alter.'
9 Therefore King Darius signed the written decree."

Now Daniel of course would pray to God on a daily
basis - he knew of this new law but continued to pray
and worship God. Once caught on this act, his
enemies promptly accused him before the king who
had no choice but to reluctantly order Daniel to be
thrown into the Lion's den. The king was deeply
grieved over having to do this - and he tried all day to
grant clemency to Daniel, but was unable.

Daniel 6:11-16

11 "Then these men assembled and found Daniel praying and
making supplication before his God.
12 And they went before the king, and spoke concerning the
king's decree: "Have you not signed a decree that every man
who petitions any god or man within thirty days, except you, O
king, shall be cast into the den of lions?" The king answered and
said, "The thing is true, according to the law of the Medes and
Persians, which does not alter."
13 So they answered and said before the king, "That Daniel, who
is one of the captive from Judah, does not show due regard for
you, O king, or for the decree that you have signed, but makes
his petition three times a day."
14 And the king, when he heard these words, was greatly
displeased with himself, and set his heart on Daniel to deliver
him; and he labored till the going down of the sun to deliver

him.

15 Then these men approached the king, and said to the king, "Know, O king, that it is the law of the Medes and Persians that no decree or statute which the king establishes may be changed."

16 So the king gave the command, and they brought Daniel and cast him into the den of lions. But the king spoke, saying to Daniel, "Your God, whom you serve continually, He will deliver you."

Now King Darius definitely feared, and respected the God of Daniel, and some bible scholars believe that he was actually the son or step-son of Queen Esther through King Ahasuerus. Queen Esther was the Jewish woman who was in exile as a slave in Persia, who later became Queen and managed to save the Jews from extermination under the evil governor - Haman of Persia (modern day Iran). Read the full account in the book of **Esther**. This would explain the great anguish and remorse that Darius felt over the law that condemned Daniel to the Lion's den. This is also why the king reassured Daniel that his God would rescue him, before the king excused himself to his palace quarters to fast.

Daniel 6:16-19

*"So the king gave the command, and they brought Daniel and cast him into the den of lions. But the king spoke, saying to Daniel, **"Your God, whom you serve continually, He will deliver you."** Then a stone was brought and laid on the mouth of the den, and the king sealed it with his own signet ring and with the signets of his lords, that the purpose concerning Daniel might not be changed.*

*Now **the king went to his palace and spent the night fasting; and no musicians were brought before him. Also his sleep went from him.**"*

As we read, the king spent the whole night awake and fasting for Daniel, and early in the morning he ran like an eager child to the Lion's den, **and this is what happens**…..

Daniel 6:19-21

*"Therefore, the king arose very early in the morning at dawn and went in haste unto the den of lions. And when he came to the den, he cried loudly with a sad voice unto Daniel; and the king, in speaking to Daniel said, Daniel, **servant of the living God, has thy God, whom thou serves continually, been able to deliver thee from the lions**?"*
Daniel responds as follows:

Daniel 6:24-23

21 "Then Daniel said to the king, "O king live forever!
*22 **My God sent His angel and shut the lions' mouths,** so*
that they have not hurt me, because I was found innocent before Him; and also, O king, I have done no wrong before you."
23 Now the king was exceedingly glad for him, and commanded that they should take Daniel up out of the den. So Daniel was taken up out of the den and no injury whatever was found on him, because he believed in his God."

Then king Darius honors God:

Daniel 6:24-27

24 "And the king gave the command, and they brought those men who had accused Daniel, and they cast them into the den of lions—them, their children, and their wives; and the lions overpowered them, and broke all their bones in pieces before they ever came to the bottom of the den.
25 Then King Darius wrote: To all peoples, nations, and languages that dwell in all the earth: Peace be multiplied to you.

26 *I make a decree that in every dominion of my kingdom men must tremble and fear before the God of Daniel. For He is the living God, and steadfast forever; His kingdom is the one which shall not be destroyed,* and His dominion shall endure to the end.

27 He delivers and rescues, and He works signs and wonders in heaven and on earth, who has delivered Daniel from the power of the lions"

So Daniel prospered during the reign of Darius and his successor Cyrus (Daniel 6:28).

The Message behind Daniel Chapter 6

So the message of **Daniel 6** is that those who try to destroy God's people, particularly when they are performing service to God will perish in their own vices, like Daniel's accusers who met their end inside the lion's den. Everything and everyone will bear their brand of fruit in the end! The good will become better and the evil will grow even more evil.

While king Darius was not above the law, **God almighty is above all laws**, and this is why Daniel who was convicted and sentenced to death under mans corrupted laws did not die at the hands of the lion's. Also the incorruptible spirit of Daniel's three friends protected them from the fiery furnace, because **the incorruptible CANNOT be burned by the fire** (1 Cor. 3).

Chapter 7 - Daniel's Dream of the "Four Great Beasts"

In chapter 7 and beyond we no longer read and learn about dreams of the kings and rulers, but of the dreams and visions of Daniel; primarily visions for the last days - for our generation. It's as if Daniel was just being prepared when he was interpreting the kings dreams, because he was about to receive some extremely complex and troubling dreams and visions about the future 2,500 years and about the end of this age.

His first vision consists of four beasts. Although they are 4 beasts the sum total of their heads are seven, just like the beast of Revelation 17.

Revelation 17:3

"*So he carried me away in the Spirit into the wilderness. And I saw a woman sitting on a scarlet beast which was full of names of blasphemy, having* **seven heads** *and ten horns.*"

The difference here is that whereas in Daniels time the beasts represent 4 kingdoms throughout the age, John's vision in Revelation is of just one beast, because it is referring to the last kingdom which will reign during the Apocalypse and which will be stronger and even more **degenerate and evil** than all the other kingdoms before it - combined!

Daniel 7:2

"*Daniel spoke, saying, "I saw in my vision by night, and behold,* **the four winds of heaven were stirring up the Great Sea**.*"

Note:

Regarding the verse *"the four winds of heaven fought the great sea"* in **Daniel 7:2**, the number four symbolizes God's divine interventions, and love. (i.e. the 4 gospels, 4 chariots and spirits of the heavens of Zechariah 6:1-5, the 4 creatures in heaven in Revelation 4, and the 4 horsemen of the apocalypse).

Daniel 7:3-4

"And four great beasts came up from the sea, each different from the other. The first was like a lion, and had eagle's wings. I watched till its wings were plucked off; and it was lifted up from the earth and made to stand on two feet like a man, and a man's heart was given to it."

This image has a dual meaning. The lion and eagle are symbols of nobility. First it is representative of the Babylonian empire which was ruled by just one man who was above the law of the land (thus the words "a man with a man's heart). It also can be applied to the last kingdom that will reign at the time of the end; which will also be ruled by one man who will also be above the law, and whose kingdom is referred to as "Babylon the Great".

Just like Babylon collapsed because of its unrepentant king, fallen mankind and his beast kingdom will also collapse during the apocalypse due to its unrepentant hearts. So this image is also a depiction of fallen man, and all of his fallen nations which in their arrogance want to do things according to their unquenchable desires and to not be held accountable to the righteous laws of God.

Daniel 7:5

"And suddenly another beast, a second like a bear. It was raised up on one side, and had three ribs in its mouth between its teeth. And they said thus to it: 'Arise, devour much flesh!'

The second beast was like a bear, with 3 ribs between its teeth, which devoured much flesh. This bear has an insatiable appetite to eat flesh. This second beast has dual meanings as well, of which the primary one is that the fleshly carnal desires of man will continue to grow into a great beast with an insatiable desire for unabated sin.
We see this in many cases of criminals that start out with petty theft or the killing of small animals, and gradually the unrepentant ones go on to commit greater and greater atrocities such as the serial killing of innocent people. Their corrupted soul actually enjoys committing these atrocities, and in the end it becomes like a drug that they cannot live without! They become beasts both figuratively and spiritually. Remember, God sees things as they are in man's innermost heart, whereas man judges others outwardly.

We will also see the aforementioned level of depravity during the coming tribulation period, whereby the unrepentant beast-like inhabitants of the earth will side with the kingdom of Satan and will curse God and his kingdom.

Revelation 16:9

"And men were scorched with great heat, and they blasphemed the name of God who has power over these plagues; and they did not repent and give Him glory."

Some bible scholars have felt that this beast is indicative of Russia, whose national symbol is that of a bear. They believe that this nation may someday revert back to the desires of being the strong arm of the world that it held prior to the cold war. As I write this book, we are beginning to see signs of the awakening bear as Russia has begun to threaten Ukraine.

Going back to this second beast which **_"was like a bear, with 3 ribs between its teeth"_** it is interesting that we also read in **Daniel 7:8** how the end time beast kingdom **will subdue 3 horns (nations)**. Obviously we can only guess at this moment which are those three nations - until it starts to play out. But the latter suggests that it may be part of the final war that occurs during the apocalypse - World War III.

Daniel 7:6

"After this I looked, and there was another, like a leopard, which had on its back four wings of a bird. The beast also had four heads, and dominion was given to it."

The third beast was like a tiger with four heads and four wings of a foul, and power was given unto it. This is representative of the third major kingdom - the Grecian empire, under Alexander the Great. This great king was like a Tiger who aggressively conquered most of the world of his day.

The Grecians were the most democratic empire of its time. It is important to know that democracy is only good when the leaders and the people operate under the rule of God's laws. Once they become void of God's laws, all democracies eventually deteriorate from within and collapse! We saw this with the Grecian and also with the last of the great empires, the Roman empire (which is representative of the forth beast below). This will also happen to the world government of the last days.

Like the four heads of the tiger, eventually Alexander the Greats kingdom would collapse and be divided into four parts (four separate kingdoms - which became weak and full of confusion).

As you will see with the next beast as well - it is important to know that duality plays a significant role in many of the prophecies in the bible. If you do not understand this concept - then you will be thoroughly confused. Once you grasp this concept then you will know that history does indeed repeat itself; it is a spiritual law for our age.

Daniel 7:7

"After this I saw in the night visions, and behold, a fourth beast, dreadful and terrible, exceedingly strong. It had huge iron teeth; it was devouring, breaking in pieces, and trampling the residue with its feet. It was different from all the beasts that were before it, ***and it had ten horns.****"*

The forth beast was dreadful and exceedingly strong with great iron teeth, and it had ten horns. This beast is a symbol of the Roman Empire which would follow the Grecian Empire. Like the iron teeth, the Roman Empire had many laws that it would enforce fiercely, with the iron teeth of its great military.
But it is probably more indicative of the final kingdom that will rule on earth in the last days - which will also have ten horns as we read below.

Revelation chapter 17:3

*"So he carried me away in the Spirit into the wilderness. And I saw a woman sitting on a scarlet beast which **was full of names of blasphemy, having seven heads and ten horns**."*

Daniel 7:8:

"I was considering the horns, and there was another horn, a little one, coming up among them, before whom three of the first horns were plucked out by the roots. And there, in this horn, were eyes like the eyes of a man, and a mouth speaking pompous words."

Horns symbolize power - so the ten horns of the beast of Daniel and Revelation signify absolute power. The beast empire has eyes of a man, meaning that the beast and fallen man both see things in the carnal manner and not like God sees things. It will also be led by an arrogant, pompous man, who will be exceedingly worse than the kings of the empires that precede his.

Important Note: It is apparent from these prophecies and the others sprinkled throughout the bible, that this last kingdom will somehow be connected to the vast area that the Roman Empire occupied and controlled during its peak. So the beast kingdom most likely will have the most power and influence in this same area. Most likely its headquarters will be based somewhere in this area. I expound on this in my new book: *"**Revelation Mysteries Decoded**: unlocking the Mysteries of the coming Apocalypse."*

Daniel 7: 9-10

"I watched till thrones were put in place, and the Ancient of Days was seated; His garment was white as snow, and the hair of His head was like pure wool.
His throne was a fiery flame, its wheels a burning fire; a fiery

stream issued and came forth from before Him.
A thousand thousands ministered to Him; ten thousand times ten thousand stood before Him. The court was seated, and the books were opened."

Daniel 13-14

"I was watching in the night visions, and behold, One like the Son of Man, coming with the clouds of heaven!
He came to the Ancient of Days, and they brought Him near before Him.
Then to Him was given dominion and glory and a kingdom that all peoples, nations, and languages should serve Him.
His dominion is an everlasting dominion, which shall not pass away, and His kingdom the one which shall not be destroyed."

The above verses speak of the Throne of God, and His Kingdom.

Daniel 7:11-12

"I watched then because of the sound of the pompous words which the horn was speaking; I watched till the beast was slain, and its body destroyed and given to the burning flame. As for the rest of the beasts, they had their dominion taken away, yet their lives were prolonged for a season and a time."

In the above passage, we have assurance that God's kingdom will soon overthrow, destroy and replace the coming beast empire - which in the end will be sent to the Lake of Fire which is a **permanent** destruction. This is also made clear in the following verse from the last book of the bible.

Rev. 19:20

*"Then the beast was captured, and with him the false prophet who worked signs in his presence, by which **he deceived those who received the mark of the beast** and those who **worshiped his image**. These two were cast alive into the **lake of fire** burning with brimstone."*

The kingdom of God will then be handed over to His saints - those who persevered and believed in Him and kept His word.

Daniel 7:13

*"I was **watching in the night visions**, and behold, one like the Son of Man, coming with the clouds of heaven! He came to the Ancient of Days, and they brought Him near before Him."*

Note how Daniel observes a vision in **utter darkness**. These night visions, symbolize the reign of man on earth which gradually degrades to total darkness (total sin) just before the return of the Lord, to re-establish the light. This **Son of Man** is Jesus; when He returns He will restore the light to the earth which at the end times will be enveloped in total darkness (total sin).

Daniel 7:15-16

"I, Daniel, was grieved in my spirit within my body, and the visions of my head troubled me. I came near to one of those who stood by, and asked him the truth of all this. So he told me and made known to me the interpretation of these things"

Note: understandably, Daniel was troubled to the point of being broken physically and spiritually. But naturally, he was also astonished by this vision, and he wanted to understand the meanings behind these visions.

Daniel 7:17-18 The four great beasts are then identified as the four kingdoms that shall arise on earth during this age, as follows:

*"Those great beasts, which are four, are four kings which arise out of the earth. **But the saints of the Most High shall**

*receive the kingdom, and possess the kingdom forever,
even forever and ever.*"

Obviously the visions that Daniel had observed were
devastating to his spirit. Imagine how devastated we
will all feel when we witness the iniquity and actually
experience the horrors of the end of day events that
Daniel saw, as they unfold before our very eyes. As I
write this, I actually feel unsettled and I will therefore
take a break.

Folks, we need to get spiritually ready today for the
time of the end!

Getting back to these passages, Daniel is given the
bad news first and then the angel attempts to
reassure Daniel with the good news. We see how kind
and merciful God is. This is how we all must be when
dealing with our fellow man.

Daniel 7:19-24:

*19 "Then I wished to know the truth about the fourth beast,
which was different from all the others, exceedingly
dreadful, with its teeth of iron and its nails of bronze, which
devoured, broke in pieces, and trampled the residue with its
feet;
20 and the ten horns that were on its head, and the
other horn which came up, before which three fell, namely, that
horn which had eyes and a mouth which spoke pompous words,
whose appearance was greater than his fellows.
21 I was watching; and the same horn was making war against
the saints, and prevailing against them, until the Ancient of Days
came, and a judgment was made in favor of the saints of the
Most High, and the time came for the saints to possess the
kingdom.
22 "Thus he said: 'The fourth beast shall be a fourth kingdom on*

earth, which shall be different from all other kingdoms, and shall devour the whole earth, trample it and break it in pieces.
23 The ten horns are ten kings who shall arise from this kingdom. And another shall rise after them; he shall be different from the first ones, and shall subdue three kings.

The empire or kingdom that will reign during the apocalypse, will have ten heads just like the great statue in the first dream, which had ten toes of iron mixed with clay. Again, this symbolized a kingdom that was unstable and corrupted. Also the other beast that John saw in Revelation had seven heads. Seven is the number of completion, so it is inferring that all the nations of the world will be complicit with - or a part of the beast kingdom. God's judgment will therefore be upon all nations - not just a handful as some may think. The influence of **Babylon the great** at the time of the end will encompass the whole world. This is why Daniel was so troubled, and why we should be too.

Daniel 7:25

"And he shall speak great words against the most High and shall break down the saints of the most High and think to move the times and the law; and they shall be given into his hand until a time and times and half a time."

There may be duality here at play. This refers of the Antichrist and false prophet who will reign during the last 3 1/2 years of the apocalypse, and who will persecute and martyr the saints of God during this period.

Daniel 7:26-27

"But the court shall be seated, and they shall take away his dominion, to consume and destroy it forever. Then the kingdom

and dominion, and the greatness of the kingdoms under the whole heaven, Shall be given to the people, the saints of the Most High.
His kingdom is an everlasting kingdom, and all dominions shall serve and obey Him."

These verses are assuring us that justice will prevail in the end.

Daniel 7:28

"This is the end of the account. As for me, Daniel, my thoughts greatly troubled me, and my countenance changed; but I kept the matter in my heart."

Upon the conclusion of these visions, Daniel was naturally very troubled and depressed, but he did not reject the message, as opposed to many people today who do not want to listen to, accept or receive the word of God nor any of the prophecies.

Perhaps Daniel was so distraught because he thought that these things would be occurring during his time, until the messenger of God (Gabriel) told him that these things were not for his time but for the end times (Daniel 12:4).

Message behind Daniel Chapter 7:

We see how mankind rejected the laws of God, and with the knowledge of Good and evil that they lusted for at the Garden of Eden, throughout this age mankind usurped God's authority, elevated themselves above God (just what Lucifer wanted to do before he was cast out of heaven) and mankind created their own rules and laws and methods of governing - hence the big mess that we are witnessing in the fallen world of today!

Chapter 8 - Daniel's vision of the Ram and Goat

Daniel has his 2nd great vision. The first four verses reveal a ram with two horns, one which was higher than the other, and the higher one rose last. This is referring to the kingdoms of Darius and Cyrus that would follow King Belshazzar's reign. All would reign during the time of Daniel.

Daniel 8:1-4

1 "In the third year of the reign of King Belshazzar a vision appeared to me, Daniel—after the one that appeared to me the first time.
2 I saw in the vision, and it so happened while I was looking, that I was in Shushan, the citadel, which is in the province of Elam; and I saw in the vision that I was by the River Ulai.
3 Then I lifted my eyes and saw, and there, standing beside the river, was a ram which had two horns, and the two horns were high; but one was higher than the other, and the higher one came up last.
4 I saw the ram pushing westward, northward, and southward, so that no animal could withstand him; nor was there any that could deliver from his hand, but he did according to his will and became great."

Now the Vision takes Daniel to the kingdom that follows the Media/Persian empire, the Grecian empire.

Daniel 8:5-12

5 "And as I was considering, suddenly a male goat came from the west, across the surface of the whole earth, without touching the ground; and the goat had a notable horn between his eyes.
6 Then he came to the ram that had two horns, which I had seen standing beside the river, and ran at him with furious power.
7 And I saw him confronting the ram; he was moved with rage

*against him, attacked the ram, and broke his two horns. There
was no power in the ram to withstand him, but he cast him down
to the ground and trampled him; and there was no one that
could deliver the ram from his hand.
8 Therefore the male goat grew very great; but when he became
strong, the large horn was broken, and in place of it four notable
ones came up toward the four winds of heaven.
9 And out of one of them came a little horn which grew
exceedingly great toward the south, toward the east, and toward
the Glorious Land.
10 And it grew up to the host of heaven; and it cast
down some of the host and some of the stars to the ground, and
trampled them.
11 He even **exalted himself as high as the Prince of the
host**; and by him the daily sacrifices were taken away, and the
place of His sanctuary was cast down.
12 Because of transgression, an army was given over to the
horn to oppose the daily sacrifices; and he cast truth down to the
ground. He did all this and prospered."*

This **"He goat"** with the large horn is representative
again of Alexander the Great, who came from the
west to conquer the eastern kings. This goat
eventually is killed and divided into four pieces, just
as the Grecian empire broke apart into four separate
governments. The little horn in verse 9 is
representative of one of the Grecian generals who
entered Jerusalem and ended the daily sacrifice in a
vain last attempt to try to idolize the remnant of the
Grecian empire instead of God. Throughout this age,
man and his governments want to abolish God's laws
and instead create laws that allow them to do
whatever they want regardless if they are immoral
laws in God's eyes (i.e. abortion, same sex marriage,
etc.). The bronze belly of the giant image of
Belshazzar's first dream represents the Greek empire.

In verse 11 we read: "*He even **exalted himself as high as the Prince of the host**; and **by him the daily sacrifices were taken away**, and the place of His sanctuary was cast down.*"

So we learn that this king will exalt himself as if he were God himself. The Greeks did place their trust and faith in their government and in man. They felt that their form of government was even better than the kingdoms before them and they emphasized man's laws over God's laws. Greek philosophy placed a greater emphasis on man rather than God, infamous for the thinkers and philosophers of their time such as Aristotle and Socrates.

The bronze belly of the image symbolized the Greek empire. Interesting, bronze is the symbol of justice, and man will be judged during the apocalypse for their refusal to worship God.

Regarding the ***"taking away of the daily sacrifice"***, the Greeks eventually invaded Jerusalem and removed the daily sacrifices, as a symbol of mans desire to worship men instead of God. When man worships men he in essence is worshipping sin and Satan. Eventually fallen man will mutate into a beast, whereby those who worship God become more and more like Him, as His spirit resides in these.

Daniel 8:13-14

13 "Then I heard a holy one speaking; and another holy one said to that certain one who was speaking, "How long will the vision be, concerning the daily sacrifices and the transgression of desolation, the giving of both the sanctuary and the host to be trampled underfoot?"

*14 And he said to me, **"For two thousand three hundred days**; then the sanctuary shall be cleansed."*

This is an incredible prophecy that was fulfilled in that exact span of time! ***two thousand and three hundred years (a year for a day)*** spans the time from Alexander the Greats conquest of Jerusalem in **333 BC** to **1967** when ***Jerusalem was recaptured by the Israelites***, which is ***exactly 2,300 years!*** Keep in mind that even during the time of Jesus, Jerusalem was under the Roman Empire.

Daniel 8:15-16

15 Then it happened, when I, Daniel, had seen the vision and was seeking the meaning, that suddenly there stood before me one having the appearance of a man.
16 And I heard a man's voice between the banks of the Ulai, who called, and said, "Gabriel, make this man understand the vision."

Daniel hears a voice, Jesus (a man's voice) authorizing the angel Gabriel to explain these visions to Daniel who like many of us today even in these last days still remain quite confused over these very detailed and complex prophecies. It is possible that the angel was withholding the unveiling of the prophecies because he knew they were end time prophecies that would occur thousands of years later (over 2,500 years later), for our generation!

Daniel 8:17-19

17 "So he came near where I stood, and when he came I was afraid and fell on my face; but he said to me, "Understand, son of man, that the vision refers to the time of the end."
18 Now, as he was speaking with me, I was in a deep sleep with my face to the ground; but he touched me, and stood me upright.

19 And he said, "Look, I am making known to you what shall happen in the latter time of the indignation; for at the appointed time the end shall be."

Again the angel is explaining to Daniel that the visions that are to now be revealed are for the last days. The deep sleep referred to in **verse 18** may infer that Daniel may have fainted from the awesome presence of the angel and his visions.

Daniel 8:20-23 - Now the angel explains to Daniel the following (which was already interpreted for you earlier in this chapter):

20 "The ram which you saw, having the two horns—they are the kings of Media and Persia.
21 - And the male goat is the kingdom of Greece. The large horn that is between its eyes is the first king.
22 - As for the broken horn and the four that stood up in its place, four kingdoms shall arise out of that nation, but not with its power.
23 - And in the latter time of their kingdom, when the transgressors have reached their fullness,
A king shall arise, Having fierce features, who understand sinister schemes."

Daniel 8:24
"His power shall be mighty, but not by his own power; he shall destroy fearfully, and shall prosper and thrive; he shall destroy the mighty, and also the holy people."

This verse is referring to the end time dictator and beast kingdom which will attempt to destroy all mankind, although he will first go after the Christians and Jews as scapegoats - to hide his real objective (to destroy all mankind)!

In the end, just like Nazi Germany, his kingdom will be utterly destroyed. But I believe that those faithful few with an incorruptible spirit will indeed be protected like the three Hebrew boys who came out of the fiery furnace unscathed.

Daniel 8:25

"Through his cunning He shall cause deceit to prosper under his rule; and he shall exalt himself in his heart. He shall destroy many in their prosperity. He shall even rise against the Prince of princes; ***but he shall be broken without human means****."*

NOTE:

This end time ruler appointed by Satan himself will be very cunning (Shrewd, sneaky), just like his father the devil. This leader of the final beast kingdom will even wage war against God's people and God himself when he attempts to invade and destroy the Holy Land **(Ezekiel 38:22-23**; Revelation 12:17). But he will be destroyed not by the armies of man, but by God Himself (Ezekiel **Revelation 20**).

Let's read **Ezekiel 38:22-23** as this important piece of the end time puzzle explains how the end time ruler and his kingdom will be destroyed "without human hands":

*"22 And **I will** bring him to judgment with pestilence and bloodshed; **I will** rain down on him, on his troops, and on the many peoples who are with him, flooding rain, great hailstones, fire, and brimstone.*
*23 Thus **I will** magnify Myself and sanctify Myself, and **I will** be known in the eyes of many nations. Then they shall know that I am the Lord."* **Ezekiel 38:22-23**

Daniel 8:26-27 - The angel again confirms that these visions are for the last days. Notwithstanding, Daniel was physically sick for several days because of the horrors he was witnessing with these visions. There is a truth that says: "be careful what you ask for, as you might get it". This certainly applied to Daniel!

Chapter 9 - Daniel's "Seventy Weeks" Prophecy

Being related to Queen Esther (possibly her son) King Darius (whose name means preserver) was instrumental in the rebuilding of the Temple in Jerusalem. The bible can be very specific in the clues it offers when they are related to prophecy as we will see in this chapter.

Daniel 9:1-3

"1 - In the first year of Darius the son of Ahasuerus, of the lineage of the Medes, who was made king over the realm of the Chaldeans
2 - in the first year of his reign I, Daniel, understood by the books the number of the years specified by the word of the Lord through Jeremiah the prophet, that He would accomplish seventy years in the desolations of Jerusalem.
3 - Then I set my face toward the Lord God to make request by prayer and supplications, with fasting, sackcloth, and ashes."

In the first three verses above, Daniel seeks to understand the meaning of the prophet Jeremiah relative to the 70 Years. As a faithful servant of the Lord, Daniel seeks to understand the word through prayer and supplication.

In **Daniel 9:4-19** we read one of the most powerful prayers in the Old Testament. He prays as we should all pray by first confessing sin. He also unselfishly is praying for his people more than for himself. In this prayer, just like Jesus in John chapter 17, Daniel is interceding for his people, the Hebrews held captive in Babylon. When Daniel fasted he observed the ritual of fasting in sackcloth and ashes, a symbol of total self denial. Daniel confirms that forgiveness is through God's mercy and grace.

Daniel 9:20-21

21 - "Yes, while I was speaking in prayer, the man Gabriel, whom I had seen in the vision at the beginning, being caused to fly swiftly, reached me about the time of the evening offering."

God heard his prayer and He answered Daniel even before Daniel finished praying! That is how powerful his prayer was and how much God favored this man. Once again, God sent the angel Gabriel to interpret the prophecy of 70 years given by Jeremiah.

Daniel 9:24*:*

"Seventy weeks are determined For your people and for your holy city, To finish the transgression, To make an end of sins, to make reconciliation for iniquity, to bring in everlasting righteousness, to seal up vision and prophecy, and to anoint the Most Holy."

The seventy weeks above are seventy weeks of years (a day = a year, so 70 x 7 = 490 years).

Daniel 9:25

"Know therefore and understand, that from the going forth of the command to restore and build Jerusalem until Messiah the Prince, there shall be seven weeks and sixty-two weeks; the street shall be built again, and the wall, even in troublesome times."

The above is one of the most important passages (a prophetic message from God) and prophecies of the entire bible, as it not only reveals that the temple will be rebuilt, but identifies who the Messiah will be, based on when he will arrive on earth, based on a specific timeline!

Shortly after Daniel received this message King Darius issues the decree to rebuild the temple - which was completed in the first week (or 49 years) of the 70 years.

Jesus Christ would make his triumphant entrance into Jerusalem on the 69th week of the seventy weeks (of years)!

Daniel 9:27

"Then he shall confirm a covenant with many for one week; but in the middle of the week he shall bring an end to sacrifice and offering. And on the wing of abominations shall be one who makes desolate, even until the consummation, which is determined, is poured out on the desolate."

This passage is the last week (last 7 years) of the 70 week prophecy. So the first 69 weeks occur from when the decree is given to rebuild the Temple in Jerusalem until Jerusalem is destroyed at around 70 AD. **Hmmm....70 week prophecy and Jerusalem and the temple are destroyed in 70 AD**! Is it just a coincidence that the number 70 coincides?

Then the prophecy jumps almost 2,000 years to the time of the end - the last seven years of this age, also referred to as the great tribulation, tribulation period, the time of Jacob's troubles, and or the apocalypse.

Chapter 10 - Vision of the "Glorious Man dressed in Linen and the intro to the Apocalypse"

Daniel receives another message from the Lord in the third year of king Cyrus of Persia. By now some of you are probably thinking, please no more dreams and visions! Well, there is only one more - but this one is covered in the next three chapters and is specifically for the end of days. So **pay close attention as it involves our generation**.

Daniel 10:2-9

2 In those days I, Daniel, was mourning three full weeks.
3 I ate no pleasant food, no meat or wine came into my mouth, nor did I anoint myself at all, till three whole weeks were fulfilled.
4 Now on the twenty-fourth day of the first month, as I was by the side of the great river, that is, the Tigris,
*5 I lifted my eyes and looked, and behold, **a certain man clothed in linen**, whose waist was girded with gold of Uphaz!*
6 His body was like beryl, his face like the appearance of lightning, his eyes like torches of fire, his arms and feet like burnished bronze in color, and the sound of his words like the voice of a multitude.
7 And I, Daniel, alone saw the vision, for the men who were with me did not see the vision; but a great terror fell upon them, so that they fled to hide themselves.
8 Therefore I was left alone when I saw this great vision, and no strength remained in me; for my vigor was turned to frailty in me, and I retained no strength.
9 Yet I heard the sound of his words; and while I heard the sound of his words I was in a deep sleep on my face, with my face to the ground.

NOTE: The above passages are a vision that Daniel is having of a glorious man (Jesus himself through the angel Gabriel).

10 Suddenly, a hand touched me, which made me tremble on my knees and on the palms of my hands.
11 And he said to me, "O Daniel, man greatly beloved, understand the words that I speak to you, and stand upright, for I have now been sent to you." While he was speaking this word to me, I stood trembling.
12 Then he said to me, "Do not fear, Daniel, for from the first day that you set your heart to understand, and to humble yourself before your God, your words were heard; and I have come because of your words.

As the vision progresses Daniel is greatly weekend and is in fear by the awesome glory of this figure so the angel touched Daniel to strengthen him, and reassure him.

Daniel 10:13:

"But the prince of the kingdom of Persia withstood me twenty-one days; and behold, Michael, one of the chief princes, came to help me, for I had been left alone there with the kings of Persia."

Important Note: The prince of the kingdom of Persia that withstood Gabriel for 21 days was a very powerful fallen angel of Satan, which is referred to as a **"prince"**. Satan assigns certain powerful fallen angels to cause havoc and stir up strife in strategic areas and nations throughout the globe. Most assuredly, the region of Persia, now modern day Iran, is a strategic nation for the prince of darkness, so Satan most likely has one of his most powerful principalities assigned to Persia. Interesting how throughout history Persia/Iran (and many of the surrounding Muslim nations) persists among Israel's greatest sworn enemies.

Daniel 10:14-19

"14 Now I have come to make you understand what will happen to your people in the latter days, for the
vision refers to many days yet to come."
15 When he had spoken such words to me, I turned my face toward the ground and became speechless.
16 And suddenly, one having the likeness of the sons of men touched my lips; then I opened my mouth and spoke, saying to him who stood before me, "My lord, because of the vision my sorrows have overwhelmed me, and I have retained no strength.
17 For how can this servant of my lord talk with you, my lord? As for me, no strength remains in me now, nor is any breath left in me."
18 Then again, the one having the likeness of a man touched me and strengthened me.
19 And he said, "O man greatly beloved, fear not! Peace be to you; be strong, yes, be strong!"
So when he spoke to me I was strengthened, and said, "Let my lord speak, for you have strengthened me."

Daniel was really overcome by the presence of the Lord and the visions, and the angel had to reassure and strengthen him more than once. Interesting how Daniel, such a picture of courage and strength before man and kings, is a picture of helplessness and weakness before the manifest presence of the Lord! The messenger of God also wants Daniel to be alert so that he can understand the message.

Note: The fact that Satan through his prince (fallen angels) did not want the angel to give these visions to

Daniel and also that the angel wants Daniel to stay alert and take careful note of the visions - is a strong indication of the importance of these messages for the end times - for our generation. So pay attention!

Daniel 10:20-21

20 "Then he said, "Do you know why I have come to you? And now I must return to fight with the prince of Persia; and when I have gone forth, indeed the prince of Greece will come.
21 But I will tell you what is noted in the Scripture of Truth. No one upholds me against these, except Michael your prince."

This vision is continued in the next chapter.

Chapter 11 - Interpretation of the Kings of North and South

Chapter 11 is a continuation of the vision of Chapter 10.

Daniel 11:1

11:1 "...Also in the first year of Darius the Mede, I, even I, stood up to confirm and strengthen him."

In the midst of fighting a powerful angel of darkness (referred to as a "prince"), apparently in charge of the area of Persia (which is modern day Iran), Gabriel (God's Archangel the chief messenger of God, who instructs His elect) is sent to Daniel to provide him some vital information for the time of the end. The angel was also in the midst of persuading king Darius of Persia to issue the decree to give the order to free the Hebrews so that they could return and rebuild the Temple in Jerusalem.

Hmmm...no wonder Gabriel was encountering so much resistance from Satan, who wants to keep God's people both ignorant and enslaved, both figuratively and literally! By the way this is not just a Hebrew story! What happens to the Jew eventually happens to all mankind, and Satan wants all mankind to be ignorant of the word, truth and to stay enslaved - in bondage to sin!

Now we must encounter and interpret some really heavy prophecy!

The following passages are some of the most detailed yet confusing and challenging prophecies in the bible. Gabriel does NOT explain this entire prophecy to Daniel because it is sealed for the time of the end (our time), meaning that no person can understand it until it actually unfolds or starts to unfold - or they receive the discernment from God.

Daniel 11:2-3

2 "And now I will tell you the truth: Behold, three more kings will arise in Persia, and the fourth shall be far richer than them all; by his strength, through his riches, he shall stir up all against the realm of Greece.
3 Then a mighty king shall arise, who shall rule with great dominion, and do according to his will.
4 And when he has arisen, his kingdom shall be broken up and divided toward the four winds of heaven, but not among his posterity nor according to his dominion with which he ruled; for his kingdom shall be uprooted, even for others besides these."

Here again we are referencing the kingdom of Alexander the Great - the Grecian Empire.

King of the North and South

To be honest with you, when I read the passages below for the first few times...I stared blankly into the heavens and muttered **- huh**? It seems like there are several messages, for several periods of times in the following passages. Let's take the passages up starting in verse five:

Daniel 11:5-19

5 "Also the king of the South shall become strong, as well as one of his princes; and he shall gain power over him and have dominion. His dominion shall be a great dominion."

6 And at the end of some years they shall join forces, for the daughter of the **king of the South** shall go to the **king of the North** to make an agreement; but she shall not retain the power of her authority, and neither he nor his authority shall stand; but she shall be given up, with those who brought her, and with him who begot her, and with him who strengthened her in those times.

7 But from a branch of her roots one shall arise in his place, who shall come with an army, enter the fortress of the king of the North, and deal with them and prevail.

8 And he shall also carry their gods captive to **Egypt**, with their princes and their precious articles of silver and gold; and he shall continue more years than the king of the North.

9 "Also the king of the North shall come to the kingdom of the king of the South, but shall return to his own land.

10 However **his sons shall stir up strife**, and assemble a multitude of great forces; and one shall certainly come and overwhelm and pass through; then he shall return to his fortress and stir up strife.

11 And the king of the South shall be moved with rage, and go out and fight with him, with the king of the North, who shall muster a great multitude; but the multitude shall be given into the hand of his enemy.

12 When he has taken away the multitude, his heart will be lifted up; and he will cast down tens of thousands, but he will not prevail.

13 For the king of the North will return and muster a multitude greater than the former, and shall certainly come at the end of some years with a great army and much equipment.

14 "Now in those times many shall rise up against the king of the South. Also, violent men of your people shall exalt themselves in fulfillment of the vision, but they shall fall.

15 So the king of the North shall come and build a siege mound, and take a fortified city; and the forces of the South shall not withstand him. Even his choice troops shall have no strength to

resist.

16 But he who comes against him shall do according to his own will and no one shall stand against him. He shall stand in the Glorious Land with destruction in his power.

17 "He shall also set his face to enter with the strength of his whole kingdom, and upright ones with him; thus shall he do. And he shall give him the daughter of women to destroy it; but she shall not stand with him, or be for him.

18 After this he shall turn his face to the coastlands, and shall take many. But a ruler shall bring the reproach against them to an end; and with the reproach removed, he shall turn back on him.

19 Then he shall turn his face toward the fortress of his own land; but he shall stumble and fall, and not be found."

Pretty heavy huh! So let's start by making some key notes and premises on Daniel 11:5-19:

a) Egypt is a symbol of man's laws, which is strife with confusion. This is why Egypt is the only nation specifically mentioned in these passages, and does not necessarily mean that Egypt will be a key player in end time prophecies, although it may indeed be the King of the South during the apocalypse.

b) The **_"he"_** that is being referred to in these passages seems to be Satan, or nations influenced or under the control of Satan; as "**_he_**" is the one who has stirred up hatred, strife, division, atrocities and wars throughout this age.

c) There also may be some cryptic prophecies intermingled within these passages that may still be unsealed until they evolve.

d) These two kings are also representative of great

empires/kingdoms or armies of nations throughout this age that will gather in the last days, just like the **"allies" and "axis"** that fought it out during **WW II.** Some scholars believe that in the last days

e) They may be referencing specific battles, wars and skirmishes throughout this age, including wars between certain regions or kingdoms that occurred in the past, and that will repeat in modern times and at the time of the end. **Remember that many of the same players participated in the first and second world war, and may also be main players during world war III** (the apocalypse).

f) In fact as we will read later in **Daniel 11:40** the term kings of the North and South is also used to describe the players during the time of the end. So the kings of the North and South are symbolic of empires, nations or groups of nations that rise up during certain times in this age to unite to participate in a major war, leading up to the battle of Armageddon.

Incorporating each of the above concepts will help you better understand the message behind these prophecies. Nevertheless, you should conduct your own research, and more importantly pray to God that he will open your eyes and ears to these and all the other prophecies in the bible.

Daniel 11:20-22

20 "There shall arise in his place one who imposes taxes on the glorious kingdom; but within a few days he shall be destroyed, but not in anger or in battle.
21 And in his place shall arise a vile person, to whom they will not give the honor of royalty; but he shall come in peaceably,

and seize the kingdom by intrigue.
22 With the force of a flood they shall be swept away from before him and be broken, and also the prince of the covenant."

The verses above appear to be prophecies of the rise of king Herod and the Roman empire in Jerusalem, at the time of Jesus Christ's birth and ministry in Israel and his subsequent death. This period would occur about 440 years after this vision (during week 69 of the 70 week prophecy). **Verse 22** may also refer to the destruction of Jerusalem in AD 70, after the crucifixion of the Messiah.

This is **also a prophecy for the last days** when the beast kingdom will once again try to invade Israel and destroy it and its covenant people just before the Lord's second return, and the end of this age! Remember, history does repeat itself - sometimes more than just once.

Daniel 11:23-35

23 And after the league is made with him he shall act deceitfully, for he shall come up and become strong with a small number of people.
24 He shall enter peaceably, even into the richest places of the province; and he shall do what his fathers have not done, nor his forefathers: he shall disperse among them the plunder, spoil, and riches; and he shall devise his plans against the strongholds, but only for a time.
25 "He shall stir up his power and his courage against the king of the South with a great army. And the king of the South shall be stirred up to battle with a very great and mighty army; but he shall not stand, for they shall devise plans against him.
26 Yes, those who eat of the portion of his delicacies shall

destroy him; his army shall be swept away, and many shall fall down slain.

27 Both these kings' hearts shall be bent on evil, and they shall speak lies at the same table; but it shall not prosper, for the end will still be at the appointed time.

28 While returning to his land with great riches, his heart shall be moved against the holy covenant; so he shall do damage and return to his own land.

29 "At the appointed time he shall return and go toward the south; but it shall not be like the former or the latter.

30 For ships from Cyprus shall come against him; therefore he shall be grieved, and return in rage against the holy covenant, and do damage. "So he shall return and show regard for those who forsake the holy covenant.

31 And forces shall be mustered by him, and they shall defile the sanctuary fortress; then they shall take away the daily sacrifices, and place there the abomination of desolation.

32 Those who do wickedly against the covenant he shall corrupt with flattery; but the people who know their God shall be strong, and carry out great exploits.

33 And those of the people who understand shall instruct many; yet for many days they shall fall by sword and flame, by captivity and plundering.

34 Now when they fall, they shall be aided with a little help; but many shall join with them by intrigue. 35 And some of those of understanding shall fall, to refine them, purify them, and make them white, until the time of the end; because it is still for the appointed time.

35 "Then the king shall do according to his own will: he shall exalt and magnify himself above every god, shall speak blasphemies against the God of gods, and shall prosper till the wrath has been accomplished; for what has been determined shall be done.

Verse 35 is reassuring, in that those who are on God's side during the time of the end will be able to continue

His ministry despite the controls of the beast kingdom. But we are certain that the 144,000 having the seal of God in their forehead are surely promised divine protection.

36 "And the king shall do according to his will."

The end time king will deploy all his power so that he can do whatever he wishes; a sign of lawlessness via a lawless ruler - a beast of sorts. Fallen man also believes that they are gods, and have thus rejected the God of heaven, His word, and His laws.

37 "He shall regard neither the God of his father's nor the desire of women, nor regard any god; for he shall exalt himself above them all."

It is hard for many of God's people, let alone for fallen man, to accept that in the last days the world will be so demon possessed that it will hate and reject the God of their fathers and fore-fathers (the God of heaven). They will reject everything that has to do with God; including the bible, the true church, Jesus Christ, the Holy Spirit, and God Himself. Instead, they will embrace everything Satan and that is why John in Revelation who is observing this corrupted end time kingdom refers to it as a beast, and the inhabitants of the earth who worship the beast as spiritual beasts as well. This is exactly what the book of Revelation reveals. They will all be blotted out of the "Book of Life" (they are sentenced to eternal damnation), because they choose to worship Satan and curse the God of heaven (read **Revelation: 13:8, 16:9 and 16:11**).

Once their soul is totally void of the Holy Spirit of God, the vacuum must be filled, and it will be filled with the opposite spirit - the evil demon filled spirit of Satan. This is why they "blindly" worship and follow the prince of darkness, the false prophet and one world dictator of Revelation 13.

The fact that he does not care for the God of his fathers, nor love of woman, or any gods means that he is incapable of any love - period. He represents complete evil.

If some want to claim that this means he is a homosexual, or celibate, is not the important point here. Rather, it is that **he cannot Love at all!** He will be Just like Satan, who cannot love, because Satan only hates, maims, and inflicts suffering. Just like the serial killers, and all those who embrace violence and hatred; they only love hatred and evil, and take great pleasure in watching others suffer - they are **_BEASTS_**!

38 "But in their place he shall honor a god of fortresses; and a god which his fathers did not know he shall honor with gold and silver, with precious stones and pleasant things."

At first the false prophet will persuade the inhabitants of the earth with his seductive gentle charisma. Then he will change and reveal his true nature - but by then it will be too late for all those that were tricked into taking his mark. BTW, "the inhabitants of the earth" is the term used in Revelation for those void of the Holy Spirit in the last days - otherwise they would be referred to as man, people or mankind.

39 "Thus he shall act against the strongest fortresses with a foreign god, which he shall acknowledge, and advance its glory; and he shall cause them to rule over many, and divide the land for gain."

Apparently this coming world religion will have some teeth, just like the Roman Catholic Church had during the dark ages. In his cunning ways, at first he will fabricate a religion that many will embrace - perhaps a new age version mixed with the popular religions of this "modern" age. After all, that is why the one world religion of the last days is referred to as a Harlot, a prostitute religion; because it embraces many religions (**Revelation 17**).

Then suddenly, this clever beast will discard or modify the one world religion to make him its sole deity; most likely after he gains enough power to force the world to worship ONLY him through his false religion at the risk of execution by the sword (just like Hitler and the Cesar's of Rome required their citizens to worship only them).

*40 "**At the time of the end** the king of the South shall attack him; and the king of the North shall come against him like a whirlwind, with chariots, horsemen, and with many ships; and he shall enter the countries, overwhelm them, and pass through."*

So we can see here that the king of the South actually still exists during the time of the end. This proves my point that the kings of the North and South are symbolic of empires, nations or groups of nations (as is in this case) that rise up during certain times in this age to engage in major wars.

As I write this book in 2014, I see great division throughout the world, and the nations are forming alliances that may lead to kings of the North and South alliances to resurface once again.

*41 "He shall also enter the Glorious Land, and
many countries shall be overthrown; but these shall escape from
his hand: Edom, Moab, and the prominent people of Ammon."*

This end of day event is very significant and is referenced is several other scriptures, as this may be the famed battle of Armageddon during the apocalypse - when the King of the North attempts to invade and destroy Israel. We read of this in more detail in Ezekiel 38 (which even names some of the countries that make up the king of the North nations).

42 He shall stretch out his hand against the countries, and the land of Egypt shall not escape.

"He" in this case may be God Himself who will stretch out His hands and He will war against the nations that come to destroy His Holy land and his covenant people. This is revealed in the following passage:

Ezekiel 38:22-23

*"And I will bring him to judgment with pestilence and bloodshed; I will rain down on him, on his troops, and on the many peoples who are with him, flooding rain, great hailstones, fire, and brimstone. Thus **I will magnify Myself and sanctify Myself**, and I will be known in the eyes of many nations. **Then they shall know that I am the Lord**."*

What a shame that God has to magnify and sanctify **Himself** because he sees such few worthy servants within the peoples of the earth!
It requires massive calamities before even those people who believe in a higher power, to finally acknowledge and bow down and worship the only God of the universe!

Ezekiel 38:43

"He shall have power over the treasures of gold and silver, and over all the precious things of Egypt; also the Libyans and Ethiopians shall follow at his heels."

The **_"he"_** in the verse above relates to the king of the North, apparently controlled by Satan since Libya and Ethiopia are part of the nations that invade Israel in the last days. The switching back and forth here is indicative of the great power struggle between the forces of good and evil that will be greatly involved in the end time battle; Satan's forces (fallen angels, demons and the nations that they influence), and God's forces (God, angels, and the nations that He influences). Revelation makes it clear that this last war will literally unleash hell on earth!

44 But news from the east and the north shall trouble him; therefore he shall go out with great fury to destroy and annihilate many.
45 And he shall plant the tents of his palace between the seas and the glorious holy mountain; yet he shall come to his end, and no one will help him.

Regarding verse 44, we obviously do not know yet what the news from the east and north shall be that causes the ruler of the beast kingdom (man of perdition) to worry.

However regarding verse 45, the man of perdition who will reign at the time of the end, he will eventually and temporarily occupy the holy mountain and perhaps may make his headquarters in Jerusalem. But this will be short lived as his beast kingdom will be short lived - about three and one half years.

Chapter 12 - Prophecies for the End of Days

As we continue with Daniel's last vision for these very last days that we are living, we begin with a warning of how bad it well get during the tribulation period (end of days, apocalypse, etc.).

Daniel 12:1

"At that time Michael shall stand up, the great prince who **stands watch over the sons of your people**; *and there shall be a time of trouble,* **such as never was since there was a nation**,
Even to that time. And at that time your people shall be delivered, everyone who is found written in the book."

This is clearly referring to the end of day scenario as it relates to Israel, called the "time of Jacob's troubles", just before the Lord's return. We can also read a very similar and much more vivid description in Revelation 16:17-18 when the final judgment bowl is poured upon the earth. While Daniel 12:1 applies primarily to the nation of Israel in the last days, the following passage applies to the entire world at the time of the end.

Revelation 16:17-18

"Then the seventh angel poured out his bowl into the air, and a loud voice came out of the temple of heaven, from the throne, saying, "It is done!" [18] *And there were noises and thunders and lightning; and there was a great earthquake, such a mighty and great earthquake* **as had not occurred since men were on the earth**."

Back to Daniel 12:1
"And at that time your people shall be delivered, everyone who is

found written in the book."

This verse promises to all of us who are written in the **Lambs Book of Life**, that we shall be delivered to paradise, at the appointed time. Understand that we are all written in the Lambs Book of Life at the moment of our inception, and at birth. However some have their name blotted out of the book based on how they choose to live.

The ***"Good News"*** (which is the meaning of the **Gospels**) is that everyone has the opportunity to have their name re-written in the Book of Life at the moment they repent and accept the redemptive blood of the Lamb of God that washes away the sins of the world - Jesus Christ! Once you do this and are thus "***born again***" into the family of God, you are automatically written in the **Lambs Book of Life** - it is your free ticket to paradise!

Daniel 12:2

"And many of those who sleep in the dust of the earth shall awake, Some to everlasting life,
Some to shame and everlasting contempt."

The above passages are referring to the <u>"Great White Throne judgment"</u>, also referred to by many as <u>*"judgment day".*</u> We get a much more descriptive passage of this monumental event in Revelation. Let's read:

Revelation 20:11-15

*11 "Then I saw a **great white throne** and Him who sat on it, from whose face the earth and the heaven fled away. And there was found no place for them.*
12 And I saw the dead, small and great, standing before God, and books were opened. And another book was opened,

which is the Book of Life. And the dead were judged according to their works, by the things which were written in the books.
13 The sea gave up the dead who were in it, and Death and Hades delivered up the dead who were in them. And they were judged, each one according to his works.
14 Then Death and Hades were cast into the lake of fire. This is the second death.
15 And anyone not found written in the Book of Life was cast into the lake of fire."

Daniel 12:3

"Those who are wise **shall shine like the brightness of the firmament**, and those who turn many to righteousness **Like the stars forever and ever**."

The verse above, promises magnificent things to those who refuse to become part of the beast kingdom and who lead others to the Lord.

Daniel 12:4

4 "But you, Daniel, shut up the words, and seal the book until the time of the end; many shall run to and fro, and **knowledge shall increase**."

This verse above provides a very significant clue that we have indeed arrived at or are very near the time of the end of this age.
The **technology boom** that this generation has enjoyed, and the rate of innovation is miraculous in its own. Just 25 years ago almost nobody had cell phones or personal computers!   People needed to buy Encyclopedias just to obtain some knowledge. Today they have both and it fits in the palm of the hand!

Today the **"many shall run to and fro, and knowledge shall increase"** pretty much describes how fast we can get information and knowledge -

pretty much instantly; as fast as you can type or speak. Today we can accomplish many tasks at lightning speed. Our fingers do the running for us to accomplish many of the tasks that we had to run around before to do. We can bank online and email others instead of having to run to the bank or to the post office. We can book our tickets online instead of running to the travel agency. We can buy books, clothing and just about anything else online without having to run to the store or mall, and so forth.

Daniel 12:5

5 "Then I, Daniel, looked; and there stood two others, one on this riverbank and the other on that riverbank.
*6 And one said to the **man clothed in linen**, who was above the waters of the river, "How long shall the fulfillment of these wonders be?"*
*7 Then I heard the man clothed in linen, who was above the waters of the river, when he held up his right hand and his left hand to heaven, **and swore by Him who lives forever, that it shall be for a time, times, and half a time; and when the power of the holy people has been completely shattered, all these things shall be finished**."*

This explains more clearly the vision that John saw which he was prevented from writing down, because the vision was sealed for the very end. It was not for John's time, but rather for another 2,000 years or so. Here is the Revelation prophecy and then we will come back to the above.

Revelation 10:5-7

5 "The angel whom I saw standing on the sea and on the land raised up his hand to heaven
*6 **and swore by Him who lives forever and ever**, who created heaven and the things that are in it, the earth and the things that are in it, and the sea and the things that are in it, that **there should be delay no longer**,*

*7 but in the days of the sounding of the seventh angel, when he is about to sound, the **mystery of God would be finished**, as He declared to His servants the prophets."*

Wow...how interesting that the verses in <u>**Daniel 12 are 5 to 7**</u>, and in <u>**Revelation 10 the verses are also 5 to 7**</u>! Is that coincidence or is it a sign that this is a very important message being offered here by the Most High for those living at the end of the age - **You and I!**
Mind you, these are two separate books written approximately 600 years apart!

When we compare the two books above, the great vision of both Daniel and John are unsealed!

Daniel 12:7 reveals that this vision will take place in approximately **2,500 years** (a time, times and half a time).

The Angel in **Daniel 12:7** and also in **Revelation 10:7** is no other than Jesus Christ because Daniel refers to Him not as an angel but as the **Man clothed in linen.** This man also was given the power to declare the end; **a power relegated to ONLY Jesus Christ in Revelation chapter four**! Obviously Daniel did not know who Jesus was since Christ had not been born yet - and so this is why Daniel refers to him as the **man clothed in linen.**

The **"There shall be no delay"** verse of **Revelation 10:6** is declaring to mankind that the end of the age and the return of the Messiah is imminent, because **"the power of the Holy people has been shattered"**. It has been shattered by the beast (Satan) and his beast kingdom (Babylon the Great), and all of his minions. There are no longer any more souls that can be saved, because the inhabitants of the earth are now totally possessed by the devil. The Holy Spirit and God's elect have now either all been removed from the earth or are at risk of all being martyred - so that there is no time left for delay!

I believe it also means that the total number of the saints has now been reached and there is no longer a reason to delay the end.

The verse **"the mystery of God will be finished"** in **Rev. 10:7** is indicative of the end of the age and the return of the Lord at which time all will be revealed to the saints!

Daniel 12:8-10

8 "Although I heard, I did not understand. Then I said, "My lord, what shall be the end of these things?"
9 And he said, "Go your way, Daniel, for the words are closed up and sealed till the time of the end.
10 Many shall be purified, made white, and refined, but the wicked shall do wickedly; and none of the wicked shall understand, but the wise shall understand."

Just like God hardened the heart of Pharaoh of Egypt repeatedly in the book of Exodus - and Pharaoh repeatedly refused to let God's people go, fallen man's heart will also be hardened at the time of the end, so that they will not understand, nor repent, nor care about their soul because they will not believe that God or Satan, or even that good or evil exists. So in their utter arrogance, they will curse God and they will refuse to let the pleasures of the world go.

While those written in the Lambs Book of Life will know the truth and are willing to die because of the truth, the inhabitants of the earth, and those who take the mark of the beast, being totally demon possessed, they will continue to sin - being blinded by their sins and they will continue to believe in the lies. The prince of darkness will keep these lost souls in the dark.

Daniel 12:11

11 "And from the time that the daily sacrifice is taken away, and the abomination of desolation is set up, there shall be one thousand two hundred and ninety days."

This verse takes us back to these last days, and so it refers to the great tribulation period which encompasses the last three and one half years of this age. This verse is revealing how the antichrist and false prophet will desecrate the Israeli temple in Jerusalem by invading it and then claiming that he is God.

Daniel 12:12

12 "Blessed is he who waits, and comes to the one thousand three hundred and thirty-five days."

God wants all of us to persevere to the end - despite the challenges. Just like Daniel persevered and accomplished a great service to God, his people, and to all mankind through the prophecies in his book, while in exile in ancient Babylon. He is the perfect model of courage, faith and loyalty for all of us who will also need to persevere while in exile in the **Babylon the great** empire of these last days!

*13 "But you, go your way till the end; for you shall rest, **and will arise to your inheritance at the end of the days**."*

For those of us who persevere to the end, and who refuse to fall prey to the false lies of protection and riches from Satan and his Babylon the Great system of the last days - this last verse promises that we will receive our inheritance, which is nothing less than eternal life as kings and priests under the King of Kings and God Almighty, forever - when we choose to side with the Lord. And God gives you that choice today!

As this last verse promises, **we will arise for our inheritance at the end of days!**

Chapter 13 - America in Prophecy, Babylon the Great, the 666, Antichrist, and More!

I believe that this is one of the most important chapters that I have written for the time of the end.

The books of Daniel and Revelation are loaded with end of day prophecies. When we study both books, we discover that they greatly complement each other, and cross referencing them helps unlock several complex prophecies. Some of the prophecies in Daniel are confusing in and of themselves, but when we read the corresponding prophecy in Revelation, it helps clarify and or unveil the prophecy.

Let's begin with some concepts to help you unlock prophecies.

Time, Dimensions and Duality

There are dual meanings for many prophecies in the bible. Many prophecies may not only apply to the generation of that prophet, but also for another generation many years in the future. Some prophecies also apply to more than two periods of time. Even with Revelation whose prophecies are for the end of days, many of those prophecies where foretold in the Old Testament, and some of the chapters in the book of Revelation cover past events that are principal causes of the apocalypse.

In order to better understand prophecies it is important to note that God operates in multiple dimensions and He is obviously not restricted by time.

This is why the verses and chapters in the books of the prophets of the bible are not in chronological order, but they jump back and forth through time sequences.

As we have discovered, many prophecies do indeed refer to more than 1 period of time and also may have more than one meaning, since history does repeat itself.

Where is America in Bible Prophecy?

Many people ask "why a revived Roman Empire and not America", or they ask "where is America in bible prophecy". I see America in many places in the bible.

As I write, America is still the most powerful nation in the world and the leader of the free world. Common sense dictates that the USA is referred to in the bible. America has certainly been greatly blessed for some of the core values that it once held. *But a nation can lose its prowess rather quickly, especially when a superpower becomes arrogant and mocks God through liberal and unrighteous laws.* As you learned in the book of Daniel, Babylon was destroyed in just one evening!

In Genesis we also read how Sodom and Gomorrah (**Genesis 19:24**) was destroyed with fire and brimstone in just one night, just like ***Babylon the Great*** will be destroyed in one hour (by fire as well) as we read in **Revelation 18**.

So Where is America in bible prophecy?

Since America did not exist during the time that the prophecies were penned, it takes some effort to unlock prophecies related to the USA, but they do exist! Let's consider for example the following passages...

Revelation 18:9-10

"The kings of the earth who committed fornication and lived **luxuriously** *with her will weep and lament for her, when they see the* **smoke of her burning**, **standing at a distance for fear of her torment**, *saying, 'Alas, alas, that* **great city** *Babylon, that mighty city!* **For in one hour** *your judgment has come.'*

Revelation 18:11

11 "And the merchants of the earth will weep and mourn over her, for no one **buys** *their merchandise anymore"*

Revelation 18:15-19

15 "The merchants of these things, who became rich by her, will stand at a distance for fear of her torment, weeping and wailing,
16 and saying, **'Alas, alas, that great city that was clothed in fine linen, purple, and scarlet, and adorned with gold and precious stones and pearls!***
17 For in **one hour such great riches** *came to nothing.' Every shipmaster, all who travel by ship, sailors, and as many as trade on the sea, stood at a distance*
18 and cried out when they saw the smoke of her burning, saying, 'What is like this great city?'
19 They threw dust on their heads and cried out, weeping and wailing, and saying, **'Alas, alas, that great city, in which all that had ships on the sea became rich by her wealth!** *For* **in one hour** *she is made desolate."*

Obviously the "**great city**" term used in **Rev. 18:19** is referring to a "**great nation**", since no city can make many merchants (nations) throughout the world rich!

<u>**It breaks my heart**</u>, but did you catch what

Revelation 18:10 is revealing?
"standing at a distance for fear of her torment, saying, 'Alas, alas, that great city Babylon, that mighty city! For in one hour your judgment has come". This passage makes it abundantly clear that Babylon the great will most likely be **_destroyed in one hour_** by means of a massive **_nuclear missile attack_**; and these merchants are observing at a distance for fear of the **_nuclear fallout_**! No dirty bombs are going to inflict such final destruction on this **_mighty_** nation.

May heavenly wisdom guide you in answering the following questions related to the passages above...

1) "What nation that exists today do you think perfectly fits the description in **Revelation 18:15-19** above?
2) Which is the wealthiest nation on earth today?
3) Which is the most powerful nation on earth today?
4) Which is the most influential nation on earth today?
5) Which nation is the greatest importer of all types of goods in the world today, which has made many nations and merchants rich, throughout the earth?
6) Which nation has leaders who have arrogantly proclaimed their nation as "the greatest nation on earth"?

Indeed, **_the USA_** does fit the description of "**_Babylon the Great_**". It could be destroyed in one hour through some kind of nuclear attack, or asteroid impact, or through some other act of man or God - **_but the passages in Revelation 18 seem to strongly suggest a nuclear event that will lead to the massive food and drinkable water shortages_**

100

prophesied in Revelation 8:7, and . .
Notwithstanding, God is not limited in ways to control or alter the destiny of nations. God is not restricted by the laws of nature, physics or mankind.

I believe America has been especially blessed because it was founded with strong Judeo-Christian values and it has always been the defender of Israel. Perhaps God has appointed America for this period of time as Israel's big brother.

In this generation however, the USA has gradually wanted to separate itself from that "big brother" role, perhaps intimidated by 9-11, or perhaps because its influence in the Mid-East region has been reduced somewhat as the nations of **Ezekiel 38** gain more control and influence in that region - in these last days.

Many things could still happen to reshape the geopolitical situation in the world and the Middle East, as nothing is absolutely certain at this time, and God is not restricted on what He can do, or how and when He does it.

So the dreaded stigma of "Babylon the great" and its corresponding curse, can be passed on from one nation to another in a relatively short span of time, if that is the will of God.

So is America "Babylon the Great"?

In Revelation 18, Babylon the great is referred to as a "*great city*" that is destroyed in one hour. As just covered, I believe that as of 2014, **Revelation 18,** and **Jeremiah 50; 51** are key chapters that eerily describe America. Unlike some bible scholars, I believe that the term "**Babylon the Great**" does not necessarily **only** refer to the end time world system and government that will prevail and be destroyed (**Revelation 18**), since Babylon will be destroyed by another entity - the beast kingdom.

The term "**Babylon the Great**" may actually dually refer to a great nation such as **America, or some other nation or group of nations such as the EU (that might perhaps also fit the description).** This great nation or group of nations will be taken out during the apocalypse by the beast, some other group of nations, terrorist groups, or by an act of God. In any case, as of 2014 I do believe that America and the European Union currently fit the description of Babylon the Great.

America which has lost its way with the supreme God of the Universe (as have all nations), through unrighteous laws over the past fifty years or so, may soon have a price to pay. All of the events that are taking place in these last days lead most prophecy scholars to believe this. Whether it merges into the beast kingdom, or is destroyed remains to be seen. Please understand that I am not pointing a finger at the USA. The bottom line is that **every nation on earth** will be adversely affected during the apocalypse, not just America.

Regardless of its role at the very time of the end, the USA could be instrumental in forming the beast kingdom (whether intentionally or not); especially since it is still the most influential nation on earth. This is why certain characteristics of "Babylon the great" as described in the prophecies (read **Jeremiah**

50 and 51, and Revelation 18) so closely resemble America which at the time of this writing is still the most powerful and influential nation on earth.

Unlike what happened in the prior world wars, Neither America, the EU, a one world government or any group of nations will be able to save the world during World War Three (the Apocalypse), their activities will actually only be carrying out Satan's dirty work of destroying all of the good that God created on earth!

The prophecies are very clear about this, and so there is no interpreting or guessing necessary. In the end, God himself will have to step in to save the world from total annihilation (**Revelation 20**), while dually cleansing the world of all its iniquity (**Revelation 16**).

By now, history should prove that neither America nor any other nation has achieved any measure of greatness on its own merits - but by the grace of God. So there is no justification for arrogance and pride as all blessings flow from the Lord! That is the message for the kings of Babylon in Daniels time, and that is the message to the daughters of Babylon the great for the end of this age (all the nations of today).

Will "Babylon the Great" be the Revived Roman Empire?

Some bible scholars believe that the Roman Empire re-emerges in the last days to become Babylon the Great; which they believe encompasses the beast kingdom, and thus is representative of all kingdoms that exist at the time of the end. They believe that it will re-emerge as part of a powerful united European Union in the last days.

I believe that this scenario actually does seem to fit somewhat into the prophecies of **Revelation 17,** but **not Revelation 18,** because neither Rome nor the EU at this time is the leader of the west, the premier global superpower, or the richest nation on earth (which all describe Babylon the great).

So if the EU evolves into the premier global power sometime from now to the time of the end, then it will more than likely be the beast nation under control of the Antichrist described in **Revelation 17** instead of Babylon the Great described in **Rev. 18**.

The reason is that the description of the woman riding the *beast with 7 heads and 10 horns* is more descriptive of a revived Roman empire which would be an aggressor rather than Babylon the Great which will be destroyed. Indeed, the beast nation does destroy Babylon the Great as alluded to in the prior section and in the manner described in **Rev. 18**.

As a side note, the remnant of the Roman Empire never really disappeared. It still exists today through all democratic nations that have incorporated the Roman governmental system such as America and many other democratic nations that have structured its laws in accordance with the Treaty of Rome. So a **revived Roman Empire** has never really been such a stretch.

So in this scenario if we include America as a part of the EU (since it is a member of NATO as well and also mutually referred to as "**the west**", then indeed the "great wealth" description of Babylon fits even better, and both **Revelation 17 and 18** would describe such a powerful end time kingdom.

Another possibility would be if America implodes economically under its enormous debt loads thus allowing another nation, or group of nations such as the European Union to assume its place as the global and economic superpower at the time of the end.

So as you can see, it is still somewhat of a moving target.

Who will destroy Babylon the Great?

We have strong indication from the bible that Babylon the Great will be a "Western" based nation (West of Israel) such as America, Western Europe, etc. It is still a bit too early to point fingers, but we have 3 possible kingdoms, those being the kings of the North, East and South as described in Daniel chapters 10, 11, and 12.

Of these three end of day kingdoms, the coming ***king of the North*** nation or group of nations will be the prime suspect (as bible prophecy reveals). The king of the North will also most likely host the antichrist, false prophet, and beast kingdom! In an upcoming book, I plan to delve much deeper in this subject as it is well beyond the scope of this book.

Why did the "Prince" attempt to stop Gabriel's final Visions for Daniel?

The prince of the kingdom of Persia that withstood Gabriel for 21 days (**Daniel 10:12-13**) was a very powerful fallen angel of Satan, which is referred to as a **"prince"**. Satan has assigned certain powerful fallen angels to cause havoc and stir up strife in strategic areas and nations throughout the globe.

105

Most assuredly, the region of Persia, now modern day **Iran**, is a strategic area, and Satan most likely has one of his most powerful principalities assigned to this region. He wants to keep his eye on **Israel**. Interesting how throughout history Persia/Iran (and many of the surrounding Muslim nations), persist as Israel's greatest sworn enemies.

The fact that Satan through his prince (fallen angel) did not want the angel to give these visions to Daniel (**Daniel 10:12-21**) and also that the angel wants Daniel to stay alert and take careful note of the visions that were forthcoming, is a strong indication of the importance of these messages for the **end times** - for our generation. Hmmm...no wonder Gabriel was encountering so much resistance from Satan, who wants to keep God's people both ignorant and enslaved, both figuratively and literally!

By the way this is not just a Hebrew story! What happens to the Jew eventually happens to all mankind. This is why **Daniel chapters 10 to 12 are prophecies of what will happen to Israel and the world from the time of Daniel to the very time of the end!**

You see, Satan wants all mankind to remain **ignorant** of the word and the truth. He wants to **keep mankind busy** with the worries and pleasures of life; and totally enslaved in bondage to Sin! This is why the prince was directed to try to keep Gabriel from revealing the future evil schemes of the enemy, and the final outcome thereof!

The end time ruler (Antichrist, also referred to as the beast, the 666) appointed by Satan himself will be very cunning (Shrewd, sneaky), just like his father the devil.

This leader of the final beast kingdom will even wage war against God's people and God himself when he attempts to invade and destroy the Holy Land **(Daniel 11:45; Ezekiel 38:22-23**; **Revelation 12:17**). But he will be destroyed not by the armies of man, but by God Himself (**Ezekiel 38:22**; **Revelation 20**).

Why would anyone take the Mark of the Beast knowing the Consequences thereof?

It is hard for many of God's people, let alone for fallen man, to accept that in the last days the world will be so demon possessed that it will hate and reject the God of their fathers and fore-fathers (the God of heaven). They will reject everything that has to do with God; including the bible, the true church, Jesus Christ, the Holy Spirit, and God Himself.

Instead, they will embrace everything Satan and that is why John in Revelation who is observing this corrupted end time kingdom refers to it as a beast, and the inhabitants of the earth who worship the beast figuratively as beasts as well. This is exactly what the book of Revelation reveals. These will all be blotted out of the "Book of Life" (they are sentenced to eternal damnation), because they choose to worship Satan and curse the God of heaven (read **Revelation: 13:8, 16:9 and 16:11**).

Once their soul is totally void of the Holy Spirit of God, the vacuum must be filled, and it will be filled with the opposite spirit - the evil demon filled spirit of Satan. This is why they "blindly" worship and follow the prince of darkness, the false prophet and one world dictator of Revelation 13.

So why would anyone take the mark?

1) Many will do it out of fear of execution or martyrdom.
2) Those with a lukewarm Spirit will be easily swayed into taking the mark.
3) Those that place their trust on their government or the media will fall for all the lies. Certainly neither the media nor the nations will be citing the prophecies, nor heeding the warnings from the word of God.
4) The many who embrace the coming False Prophet, Antichrist, and one world religion will be easy prey for the beast. Sadly everyone not written in the Lambs Book of Life will worship the beast; that is everyone not elected for salvation!

Revelation 13:8

*"**All who dwell on the earth will worship him, whose names have not been written in the Book of Life** of the Lamb slain from the foundation of the world."*

And many who do not believe or read the bible, will fail to heed the stern warning from God below, about what will happen to ALL who take the mark of the beast.

Revelation 14:

"Then a third angel followed them, saying with a loud voice, "If anyone worships the beast and his image, and receives his mark on his forehead or on his hand, he himself shall also drink of the

108

wine of the wrath of God, which is poured out full strength into the cup of His indignation. He shall be tormented with fire and brimstone in the presence of the holy angels and in the presence of the Lamb."

Who is the 666?

Like a suspenseful mystery movie, people have been looking high and low to solve the mystery of the "666" and identify who this man of perdition is or will be.

Certainly there will be one person who is also labeled as the 666 in Revelation; he is the antichrist, the man of perdition - the leader of the beast kingdom.

However, the 666 in revelation may indeed refer to the combined fallen (the unrepentant) inhabitants of the earth that will exist at the time of the end! Note that the number 6 is representative of the number of man (man was created on the sixth day). So the number 666 may be referring to the totality of fallen man! After all the unrepentant are the ones that will support, empower and feed the beast and the beast kingdom, and thus allow the antichrist and false prophet to gain the full power, influence and authority that they need to control the earth at the time of the end!

So men have been trying to unlock the mystery of 666, and all this time the enemy may have been inside of every man who refuses to worship and obey the God of the universe! In the last days the 666 will most definitely apply to all, the many millions - perhaps billions who will side with the devil and take his mark - the "**mark of the beast**"!

Once they make that covenant with the devil these lost souls will become part of the beast and this is why it will be impossible for such inhabitants to ever repent or be forgiven. Once they take that mark, it is as if they instantly inherit the DNA of the devil - so that it will be inherently impossible for these individuals to repent, to feel remorse or retain their conscience.

So do not let the 6 in the 666 be you! It will be like the unpardonable sin that Jesus warned mankind about!

Who is the Antichrist - the coming one World Ruler?

In the near future the world will experience a series of calamities, which could be from acts of God, and or manmade; such as a nuclear showdown, a global economic meltdown, or some other crisis.

Then this charismatic person will emerge onto the world scene. The Antichrist (the beast) will persuade the inhabitants of the earth with his seductive charisma to embrace his solutions to the world's problems. He will seem to have solutions for just about everything including establishing peace throughout the world, and even uniting the nations, economies, and religions into what seems to be a cohesive and effective system. The world will worship this man.

He referred to as the Antichrist, and also as the man of perdition, and the beast. He will receive his power and authority directly from Satan.
In the time of the end, he will reveal his true nature and he will require the world to worship him as god.

Incredibly most will do just that by willingly taking up his mark on their hand or forehead, referred to as the mark of the beast (**Revelation 13:16-17**). BTW, "the inhabitants of the earth" is the term used in Revelation for those void of the Holy Spirit in the last days - otherwise they would be referred to as man, people or mankind.

Revelation 13:16-17

"He causes all, both small and great, rich and poor, free and slave, to receive a mark on their right hand or on their foreheads, and that no one may buy or sell except one who has the mark or the name of the beast, or the number of his name."

Keep in mind however, that anyone who tries to destroy the body of Christ, blaspheme His name, or disrupt the advancement of His church can also be referred to as a type of Antichrist. We have seen these types throughout this age.

All who take the mark of the beast become a part of the Antichrist, since without these unrepentant and evil souls, Satan and the Antichrist would not be able to successfully execute their end time plans.

Who is the Beast?

Generally speaking the beast of Daniel and revelation refers to the **beast kingdom** or **Babylon the Great** which is the kingdom that will reign at the time of the end. In Daniel it is also referred to as the **king of the north**.

In the eyes of God however, any corrupted soul or nation is a beast. This principle helps unlock many of the visions and dreams regarding carnivorous animals

111

(beasts) referenced in many prophecies - such as bears, dragons, tigers, and lions.

Those who choose to remain in sin and to worship the things of this world are de facto, the collective beast of Revelation and these will choose to side with, worship and thus empower the devil. I believe that is why the lost souls of the world are referred to as "**the inhabitants of the earth**" instead of man because at the time of the end, these inhabitants will be so void of the word and spirit of God, that they are more like beasts than human beings!

Understand that the enormous beast of **Revelation** evolved from the tiny serpent on a tree that we read about in the Garden of Eden (Genesis 3:1) into the giant beast of Rev. 13:1, because fallen man has fed the beast during this our age with the **fuel of iniquity**. The beast grows more and more powerful every day because of man's collective sins. As the world continues to grow immorally its appetite for depravity, sin and hatred grows exponentially - until at the end of this age man surrenders to the beast and allows it to fully devour them!

So based on the state of a person's mind and soul, he or she could indeed be labeled as a beast as well, both figuratively and spiritually.

The One World Religion

Apparently this coming world religion will have some teeth, just like the Roman Catholic Church had during the dark ages. In his cunning ways, at first the false prophet, who is appointed by the antichrist, will fabricate a religion that many will embrace - perhaps a new age version mixed with the popular religions of this "modern" age. After all, that is why the **one world religion** of the last days is referred to as a Harlot (a prostitute) religion; because it mixes many religions into what God terms as an abomination. And as we will read below, **it will be a central component of the beast kingdom** (Babylon the Great).

Revelation 17:4-5

4 *"The woman was arrayed in purple and scarlet, and adorned with gold and precious stones and pearls, having in her hand a golden cup **full of abominations** and the filthiness of her fornication."*
5 *And on her forehead a name was written:*

**MYSTERY, BABYLON THE GREAT,
THE MOTHER OF HARLOTS
AND OF THE ABOMINATIONS
OF THE EARTH.**

Then suddenly, this clever beast will discard or modify the one world religion to make him its sole deity (Satan has always lusted for God's sovereignty). This will most likely occur after he gains sufficient power to force the world to worship ONLY him at the risk of execution by the sword (just like Hitler and the Cesar's of Rome required their citizens to worship only them).

Unlocking the Mystery of Angels?

An angel is an angelic spirit that serves God for many activities related to His kingdom, as well as the earth. Below is a list of just the functions that the bible has revealed that the angels perform here:

1) Angels are a **messenger of God**.
2) The **defenders** of God's people
3) **fellow-servants** of man.
4) **Warriors** against Satan, the fallen angels, demons and principalities.
5) The **release of judgments** against peoples, nations, and the world. This is made quite clear in the book of Revelation.
6) Angels are the **protector** and **guardian** of all those whom God chooses to bless, and protect.
7) Any person who is a messenger of God can be referred as an angel.

At times even the Lord takes on the form of an angel. The Angel in **Daniel 12:7** (and also in **Revelation 10:7)** is no other than Jesus Christ because Daniel refers to Him not as an angel but as the "**Man clothed in linen**". This man also was given the power to declare the end; **a power relegated to ONLY Jesus Christ in Revelation chapter four**! Obviously Daniel did not know who Jesus was since Christ had not been born yet - and so this is why Daniel refers to him as **"the Man clothed in linen".**

Angels will be heavily involved in the end of day events. The **"There shall be no delay"** verse of **Revelation 10:6** is declaring to mankind that the end of the age and the return of the Messiah is imminent, because "**the power of the Holy people has been shattered**". It has been shattered by the beast (Satan) and his beast kingdom (Babylon the Great), and all of his minions. There are no longer any more souls that can be saved, because the inhabitants of the earth are now totally possessed by the devil, and the Holy Spirit has left the scene (**Revelation 4:5**). God's elect have now either all been removed from the earth or are at risk of all being martyred - so that there is no time left for delay!

I believe it also means that the total number of the saints has now been reached and there is no longer a reason to delay the end.
So God will use His **angels** in a serious of 3 groups of seven, to exact His final judgments upon the inhabitants of the earth during the apocalypse.

The verse **"the mystery of God will be finished"** in **Rev. 10:7** is indicative of the end of this age and the return of the Lord at which time all will be revealed to the saints!

The term **"guardian angel"** may indeed be accurate. Throughout the bible we read of many instances where God has sent His angels to assist and instruct His people.

- God sent an angel to warn Joseph and Mary to leave Bethlehem in order to protect baby Jesus from execution by King Herod.

- God sent an angel to warn lot and his family and to subsequently lead them out of Sodom and Gomorrah prior to its total destruction.

- And as we have read, God sent His **archangel Gabriel** to **Daniel** on several occasions to provide crucial messages and prophecies for his time and for the time of the end.

In reality, any messenger of God, whether it is Jesus, or a prophet, is figuratively speaking of an angel.

Let's pray that God will assign an angel to shelter us from the coming Day of the Lord's anger.

Why Will the World go through the Apocalypse?

Sadly, there are many reasons and an entire book can be written as to why the world will go through the tribulation period (Apocalypse). So I will let the word of God through the prophet Isaiah offer the main reasons.

Isaiah 24:5-6

5 *"The earth is also defiled under its inhabitants, because they have* **transgressed the laws, violated the statutes, and have broken the everlasting covenant.** *Therefore a curse devours the earth and those who dwell in it are held guilty. Therefore the inhabitants of the earth are burned, and few men are left."*

Here God states that the coming calamities upon earth come because people and nations, the entire earth, refuse to follow His law, and have even tried to change it.

Is it too late to save ourselves or this world?

If you are reading this book, then it is still not too late for you,

But for unconverted mankind, the door may shut suddenly on them! That does not mean that it is too late for God to slow down the clock. God who is not restricted by time can extend time for humanity based on the prayers and actions of the peoples and nations of the world.

But there is no way out for this age, and the inhabitants of this last generation. The line has been crossed too far. As in **Daniel 5:3-5**, the writing is already on the wall. **NOT even one** of the prophecies of God in his word is going to not come to pass.

God has declared that **Babylon the Great will fall**, just like the Babylon of Daniels time fell. Just like Belshazzar mocked God by desecrating the golden vessels of the temple of Jerusalem, the world has mocked God by rejecting his sovereignty and transgressing his laws. This world cannot be saved - it will be changed. It is just a matter of time before the **following ominous passage** comes to fruition.

Isaiah 24:1-6

1 "Behold, the Lord makes the earth empty and makes it waste,
distorts its surface and scatters abroad its inhabitants.
2 And it shall be:
As with the people, so with the priest;
As with the servant, so with his master;
As with the maid, so with her mistress;
As with the buyer, so with the seller;
As with the lender, so with the borrower;
As with the creditor, so with the debtor.
3 The land shall be entirely emptied and utterly plundered,
for the Lord has spoken this word.
4 The earth mourns and fades away, the world
languishes and fades away; the haughty people of the earth
languish.
5 The earth is also defiled under its inhabitants,
because they have transgressed the laws, violated the
statutes, and have broken the everlasting covenant.
6 Therefore a curse devours the earth and those who
dwell in it are held guilty. Therefore the inhabitants of the
earth are burned, and few men are left."

As you read in the passages above - every person and every nation will be affected on that terrible day of

God Almighty, referred to as the "**Day of the Lord's Anger**", and as "**the Great Day of God Almighty**".

But for the repentant it is not too late! Submit to God today. Unless you submit to the supreme God of the universe and let go of this lost world and let God in, then it could also be too late for you very soon.

Don't Harden Your Heart

God warns people about hardening their hearts against the truth of His law (Zechariah 7:12).

Just like God hardened the heart of Pharaoh of Egypt repeatedly in the book of Exodus - and Pharaoh repeatedly refused to let God's people go, fallen man's heart will also be hardened at the time of the end, so that they will not understand, nor repent, nor care about their soul because they will not believe that God or Satan, or even that good or evil exists. So in their utter arrogance, and corrupted soul, they will curse God and they will refuse to let the pleasures of the world go.

They will allow and applaud the Martyrdom of the saints (God's people), just like they had a worldwide block party when God's two witnesses are martyred by the beast (read **Revelation 11:7-10**). This is why the inhabitants of the earth will also have to drink the blood of the wrath of God!

Revelation 16:4-6

4 "Then the third angel poured out his bowl on the rivers and springs of water, and they became blood.
5 And I heard the angel of the waters saying:
"You are righteous, O Lord, the One who is and who was and

who is to be, because You have judged these things.
6 for they have shed the blood of saints and prophets,
and You have given them blood to drink. For it is their just do."

Important point

The important take away from this chapter is that instead of trying to know who the 666, antichrist or beast kingdom is, you want to make sure your spiritual house is in order before ***all hell literally breaks loose here on earth***.

There are no prizes in God's kingdom for figuring out all of these external dynamics (although it certainly won't hurt), but rather for figuring out and then actively ***seeking the Lord*** and ***living His word***. That my friend is what matters, and it is not hidden in the bible like some mystical end time prophecy; it is clearly explained in the gospels by Jesus Himself and that is the most important message that God has for mankind in this age!

Zephaniah 2:3

*"**Seek the Lord,** all you humble of the earth, who have upheld His justice. **Seek** righteousness, **seek humility**. It may be that you will be hidden in the **day of the Lord's anger**."*

Chapter 14 - Summary - Final Lessons from Daniel

When you have the right spirit - God will listen to all your requests, just as He listened to Daniel.

There are very few patriarchs of the bible who were not blemished with sin; Daniel was one of them. There is no record of him ever having sinned, just like Joseph of Genesis, and Jesus Christ Himself. This is why when Daniel prayed, God listened and answered him.

We learned how those who serve the Lord will receive **supernatural blessings** and **protection**. Daniel desired to understand the prophecies and visions for his people and their destiny through time. Because of his righteous spirit and because he knew how to pray, God sent the angel Gabriel to bestow him with the great honor of providing for all mankind the *prophecies that lead right to the very end of this age*.

Another lesson from Daniel is that as we mature in spirit - we will become more and *more fearless*, just like Daniel in the Lion's den, or the three young Hebrew boys dancing with joy along with Jesus in the fiery furnace.

Also, we have learned that, pretty much in all the visions and dreams in the book of Daniel, the theme is that natural man is **not** evolving into some kind of superhuman form, as this fallen world wants you to believe.

Those who have separated from the Lord are mutating spiritually into what Satan wants fallen man to become - a **beast** before the eyes of God. These horrible beasts that are depicted in Daniel and Revelation are symbolic of spirits that are evil in nature, both carnal and supernatural spirits. These visions from God are depicting the soul of these beasts not their outward appearances since God judges man from his inner being and not his physical being.

And Just like God had to take Egypt out of the rebellious children of Israel, we need to take the spirit of **Babylon the Great** out of our mind, body and soul. We need to take this message seriously, because once the spirit crosses a certain line, it no longer can or wants to repent, and at that point - it must and will be destroyed.

My primary career throughout most of my adult life has been as a financial advisor and insurance sales. I probably more than most am qualified to confess to you that I have tried everything, and I served mammon just as much or perhaps even more than most. After God tore me down and built me back up I want you to know that there is no greater investment and no greater insurance in life than to commit your life to the sovereign God of the universe. Like Jonah, we want to see the light and never look back.

God appreciates that it takes a strong spirit, a special person, to keep or strive to keep His laws. The Jews failed at it and so has all mankind. God knew this would happen, so He sent His son Jesus Christ as a sacrifice, a substitute for you and me, so that through

His blood we can secure eternal life. God made it so easy that now there is just no excuse.

You too can be a special person before the eyes of God. One who embraces and appreciates the prophecies within the word of God. And since it demonstrates a greater appreciation for His word, God offers a special blessing to those who read, hear and heed the prophecies for these last days (**Rev. 1:3**).

How to be Sheltered on the Day of the Lord's Anger

My brothers and sisters in Christ, the message of the Apocalypse is bleak for the unrepentant inhabitants of the earth - but it is glorious for His elect, those of us who faithfully await the return of the Lord.

So your objective for these last days is to do everything in your spirit to **resist** the devil and his evil schemes and fiery darts. Place your trust on the Lord, put on the full armor of God (**Ephesians 6:11**) and stand firm on your Christian principles, and just like Daniel was protected in his day, **perhaps you too will be sheltered on the Day of the Lord's anger**...

Zephaniah 2:3
*"Seek the Lord, all you meek of the earth, who has upheld His justice. **Seek** righteousness, **seek humility**. It may be that you will be hidden in the day of the Lord's anger."*

Let us continue strengthened by the spirit of the sovereign God, and with a renewed life focused on the Lord and the word, having been enlightened in knowing just like **Daniel knew**, that **nothing else matters - this side of heaven!**

It has been a great blessing and a privilege for me to write this book. As your fellow servant I pray that this book has been helpful for you allowing you to have a greater appreciation for the incredible amount of divine wisdom, messages and prophecies found in the **book of Daniel**.

May God bless you richly, and may the Holy Spirit prompt you to seek His guidance, and protection in these last days.

Revelation 1:3

*"**Blessed is he who reads and those who hear the words of this prophecy**, and keep those things which are written in it; for the time is near."*

<u>Bonus Chapter</u>:

This complimentary chapter is an excerpt (chapter 7) from my brand new book published on 1/1/2015:
"***Apocalypse Countdown - 2015 to 2021***"

Chapter 7 - The Book of Revelation and the Apocalypse

While the prior chapter was date specific relative to heavenly signs and appointed feast days that could be harbingers of the apocalypse. We will now discover the events and the series of judgments that will unfold once the apocalypse begins.

The book of Revelation is appropriately the last book of the bible, because it is primarily the **go to book on the last days of this age**. It also is the revelation of Jesus Christ in that it reveals that Jesus Christ was and is the Messiah, and He will return to rule the world at the conclusion of this age of man. God allowed man 6,000 years to mess everything up and prove that **without the Spirit of God** mankind has always and will always be unable to resist the temptations of their carnal spirit which makes them susceptible to the cunning of Satan and his dark evil influences, which has and will ultimately lead this world to its demise.

To stay in topic let's review the key clues in the book of Revelation regarding the apocalypse and what types of events are revealed to take place before during and after the great tribulation period (apocalypse)

The apostle John was in exile in the Island of Patmos by the Romans because of his testimony of Jesus. While in exile, he received many visions from Jesus and some of His angels. John could only describe these visions symbolically as they were for the last days; the days that you and I live in. So the description of these visions can be quite confusing to the untrained mind. Since my book is about the time of the end I will only cover the key prophecies of Revelation pertaining to our time.

Before we begin, keep in mind that in many end time prophecies duality comes into play, representing visions and prophecies that may apply to more than one nation, time in history, and meaning. For example when one reads of Babylon, it may refer to ancient Babylon or to Babylon of the last days. With careful study and cross referencing of scriptures, you can and will correctly interpret the prophecies. With that said let's move on to the phases of judgments during the apocalypse.

Rev. Chapter 6 and 7 - Jesus has a scroll in his hand with 7 seals. When He opens the seals of the scroll - each one announces the Judgments that are to come upon the whole earth. The first four scrolls reveal the four horsemen of the apocalypse. These are not literal men riding on horses but rather they are symbolic of the events that will be unfolding during the great tribulation (apocalypse). I believe these events will occur in rapid succession one after another; hence the vision of horses in motion; one immediately after the other.

The Seven Seal Judgments

The 1st Seal is the first horse - a white horse whose rider has a bow but no arrows. This may be describing **the Antichrist** (man of perdition) that is to come, masquerading as a savior with peaceful intentions, and thus conquering an unsuspecting world through deceptive means (**Rev. 6:2**).

The 2nd Seal is the second horse - a rider on a red horse carrying a great sword to take peace from the earth, **so that people could kill one another**. This is clearly symbolizing war among the nation - perhaps **World War III** (**Rev. 6:4**).

The 3rd Seal is the third horse - a rider on a black horse carrying scales on his hand and based on what is said in this passage, it is revealing **a great famine throughout the world**; a great shortage of food supplies as a result of devastated lands due to the war released by the second seal (**Rev. 5-6**)

The 4th Seal is the fourth horse - a rider on an ashen (grayish green) horse symbolizing death and hell.   This rider is **symbolic of the beast kingdom consisting of the ten nation confederacy**. Notice that the rider is referring to "*them*" and not "*him*". It further states that "power was given to them over a fourth of the earth, to kill with sword, with hunger, with death, and the beasts of the earth." I believe this fourth rider is the final beast kingdom under control of the man of perdition that destroys 1/4th of the earth - possibly with weapons of mass destruction! I believe that the "**beasts of the earth**" is NOT referring to lions, bears and other predator animals but rather the leaders of the beast kingdom, consisting of the ten nation confederacy and the henchmen that martyr the saints as we read in the fifth seal that follows.

Note: The term "***beast***" refers to the beast kingdom and all the people that associate with it, and who worship the beast (Satan) and take his mark (the mark of the beast).

5th Seal - reveals a great persecution and Martyrdom of a myriad of saints by the beast kingdom because of their testimony/witness of the name of Jesus Christ as the son of God in accordance with the word of God, in the Holy bible. These who are referred to as "**saints**" are the Christians and elect who are beheaded or killed by other means because they do not bow down and worship the Antichrist (Satan's man of perdition), who has come to full power over the earth after the fourth seal above.

Important Note: The revelation clearly reveals that the saints (all Christians - the body of Christ) will be targeted and hated not just by the one world government but most of the inhabitants of the world who will be brainwashed into believing that the antichrist is God, and the false prophet is Jesus! That is why they will gladly take the mark of the beast. This hatred towards all witnesses of the Lord is clearly revealed in various places including **Rev. 11:10**, when the inhabitants of the earth celebrate when the two witnesses appointed by God to witness to the world in an effort to save as many souls as possible, are killed by the man of perdition (Satan's representative on earth).

6th Seal - A great Earthquake rocks the planet.

7th Seal - when the seventh seal is released, there is silence in Heaven for 1/2 hour, and seven angels are given seven trumpets in preparation of the release of the trumpet judgments of God. This appears to be a transition point, a short period of rest, perhaps to allow for some to repent before the trumpet judgments begin.

NOTE: This period of rest at the seventh seal is interesting when we consider that the Lord rested on the seventh day and sanctified it (made it Holy), and how he commands you and I to do the same. Obviously the Sabbath day was never abolished as it is symbolically observed even in heaven during the apocalypse, and it is one of the Ten Commandments (**Exodus 20:8-11**). This may be another main reason why the **seventh seal** does not release any judgments upon the earth! When you study Revelation carefully as I have, you will perceive the level of perfect precision on how even the last seven years of the age of man unfold. It is like a religious or holy ceremony in heaven commemorating the end of this imperfect age.

The first 6 seals of Revelation chapter six appear to be a synopsis of the key events that will occur during the great tribulation, which **will NOT begin** until the man of perdition is finally revealed.

Note that these seal judgments are not necessarily direct judgments from God, but rather judgments and curses that man has brought upon himself by placing their faith in man, instead of in God!

The Seven Trumpet Judgments

Now let's move on to the seven trumpet judgments:

The trumpet Judgments are sounded by seven Angels. These angels are charged with executing God's judgments; the "wrath of God judgments". We can infer from **Rev. 6:10-11** that these judgments come upon the earth in large part because of the blood of the saints (God's children, the body of Christ) that was shed because of their testimony of God's word:

1) The first angel sounded his trumpet - **which destroys all green grass, and _a third_ of all trees**. (**Rev. 8:7**). This would obviously lead to a global famine, and many millions would die of starvation.

So the **first trumpet** appears to be describing a thermonuclear attack that destroys a third of earth (Note that the western hemisphere is one third of the earth). _**A third of the trees**_ were burned up as well as all green grass. One can imagine the enormous loss of life and the magnitude of the pestilence and famine that would affect the entire earth when one third of all trees are vaporized and _**all green grass**_ (i.e. vegetation) is burned up.

2) The second angel sounds his trumpet and a great mountain falls on the sea and a third of the sea became blood. This is NOT a literal mountain or literal blood, but is John's way of describing perhaps **a large asteroid** or **nuclear missiles** that land in the ocean and contaminate one third of the ocean water. As a direct result, _**one third**_ of all sea creatures perish, and one third of the ships at sea are destroyed. Most likely tsunamis will also wreak havoc on many coastal areas (**Rev. 8:8-9**).

3) When the third angel sounds his trumpet - a great star fell from heaven burning like a torch, and this one contaminates **one third** of the rivers and springs of water, many men perish from drinking this water. This one may be caused by nuclear weapons (or again asteroids), because the description "burning like a torch" is more descriptive of an intercontinental ballistic missile (ICBM), and it contaminates drinking water, causing many people die from drinking it. Perhaps they are not aware of the level of radiation in this water thinking that the contamination is not so widespread (**Rev. 8:10-11**).

So this star is most likely one or several nuclear missiles impacting a land mass with rivers and springs of water. We also read here that a third of the earth is darkened due to this nuclear attack on an area of the globe, resulting in great death.

4) The fourth angel sounded and "*a third* of the sun, moon, and stars were struck, so that a third of them were darkened and a third of the day did not shine (**Rev. 8:12**). This must mean that one third of the earth has been devastated either by a massive asteroid impact or thermo-nuclear exchange or related catastrophe.

Make note that so far *one third* of the earth's land mass is affected by the first four trumpet blasts? God is placing great emphasis on this, which leads me to believe that the great tribulation will begin when a large land and ocean area of the world is devastated.

In **Rev. 8:13** we are warned that the next 3 trumpet judgments are going to make things even worse for the remaining inhabitants of the earth.

Note: Given the **Rev. 8:13** warning, it is hard to imagine as I write this in early December 2014, how progressively bad things will actually get. This is ***probably because at this point the restrainer is removed*** from the earth giving Satan power to wreak maximum havoc over this planet.

We should all ***pray*** that God indeed will rapture His elect - the church (the body of Christ) before the great tribulation begins, as many theologians believe (Pre-tribulation rapture)! But when we read in the revelations that a myriad (millions) of saints will be martyred during the apocalypse, one must wonder and prepare for a mid or post rapture of the saints. Regardless, we must remain prepared and ready since our appointed time to meet our maker can be at any moment.

5) The fifth angel sounds his trumpet - A Star (perhaps a fallen angel) falls from heaven and has been given the key to the bottomless pit (Hades/hell). He opens the bottomless pit and smoke arose out of the pit like the smoke of a great furnace (**Rev. 9:1-2**). This may be describing a massive volcanic eruption which also shoots out smoke just like a great furnace!

The fifth trumpet also releases evil spirits from Hades who afflict all men except the 144,000 who have the seal of God on their forehead and who have been granted special protection from God (**Rev. 9:3-11**).

The locusts that arise out of the bottomless pit as a result of the fifth trumpet could be some form of **germ warfare** or **manufactured virus** since they do not harm the vegetation but only the inhabitants of the earth; specifically those who do not have the seal of God on their forehead (i.e. the 144,000). This germ or virus apparently affects the body for five months; perhaps a vaccine is developed to curtail the pandemic. Jesus does warn in **Mathew 24**, that the end of day judgments will include pestilence and disease (such as the Ebola virus outbreak of 2014).

Note: The revelation that demons are instructed to afflict only the non-believers, should be a reminder to all that Satan is NOT even a friend to the non-believers. Satan does not discriminate, he hates anything associated with God and equally, and is bent on destroying it all and taking it all to hell with him. This includes the grass, trees, planet earth and all human beings which were all created in the image of God.

6) The sixth angel sounds his trumpet - and four *fallen* Angels which were bound at the Euphrates River are released (**Rev. 9:14-15**). These evil angelic beings were so powerful that they had to be physically restrained until this moment in time.

The Euphrates River runs through Iraq. This may be indicating that the area of Iraq (where the terror army called ISIS is presently based), and the Middle East as a whole may be ground zero for the establishment of the beast kingdom and headquarters of the man of perdition. Also interesting how this area of the Middle East has always been an area of Jewish and Christian intolerance and persecution.
These four fallen angels kill a third of mankind, with a massive 200,000,000 man army which once the demonic influences are released in that region, invade from the east.

They are able to do this by influencing an army of 200 million; this may be a continuation or beginning of World War III that was announced at the opening of the aforementioned second and fourth seals.

Note: In John's time an army that size was impossible. Today it is quite possible considering the nearly seven billion worldwide population. We also discover that this army will kill one third of mankind with the use of weapons that rain down fire and brimstone **which again reads to me like nuclear weaponry (Rev. 9:15-18**).

Rev. 9:20-21 makes it clear why these judgments continue to persist to the very end, as those who survive through all of the prior judgments still refuse to repent from worshipping demons, idols, sorcery, murder, sexual immorality and thefts.

The seventh angel sounds his trumpet and we have another break from the Judgments; ***another Sabbath break*** in between the trumpet and the final bowl judgments. Victory is proclaimed in heaven and a celebration commences as the angels and elders announce that the kingdoms of this world are now the kingdoms of the Lord; as the Messiah prepares for His triumphant second coming!

The Sabbath is to be a day where we stop all work and worship the Lord; thanking Him for the prior week's blessings. On this day we pray, nourish our spirit with the word, and develop our relationship with the Lord. We saw that after the sixth seal was released, Revelation chapter seven is an instructional chapter. Once again after the sixth trumpet judgment in Revelation chapter nine, chapter ten is also an instructional chapter right through Rev. 11 verse 14 when the seventh trumpet judgment is released.

After the seventh trumpet judgment, Revelation chapters 12 through 15 are instructional chapters as well which describe the following:

Rev. Ch. 12: This chapter covers the cosmic battle that Satan has waged against Israel, and mankind. Note that he is NO MATCH to Jesus and God, so that he can only attempt to defeat Jesus and God through mankind! ***Satan knows he already lost his battle against the Messiah almost 2,000 years ago when Jesus Christ became our sacrificial Lamb at the cross, allowing anyone who acknowledges and accepts His sacrifice the right to become children of the Most High***! Messiah has **already** earned the deed to planet earth and the universe. In His mercy He is just waiting for the full number of saved souls to be reached before He returns (**Rev. 6:10-11**)!

Rev. Ch. 13: This chapter describes the antichrist, false prophet and the beast kingdom that will reign approximately three and one half years before the second coming.

Rev. Ch. 14 and 15: are celebratory chapters in heaven whereby the angels and the saints (all those who were previously martyred because they refused the mark of Satan) prepare for the final series of judgments and the return of the Messiah to establish a new heaven and a new earth - one that is purified, and cleansed of all sin). Some scholars believe that by this point the rapture may have already occurred.

The Final Seven Bowl Judgments

Now we move on to the last series of judgments; the Bowl (also referred to as vial) judgments. Like the Trumpet judgments, the bowl judgments are also a part of the "**Wrath of God Judgments**". This series of judgments appears to be particularly for those who accepted the mark of Satan (mark of the beast), and all who refuse to repent.

1) The first Bowl is poured out and a horrible sore *afflicts all those who took the mark of the beast (Satan) and who worshiped his image*.
I hope that you like I are finding it really hard to comprehend how so many will be so deceived by Satan in these last days into thinking that this coming demon possessed one world government leader of the final one world government is God or can actually defeat and or prevent the second coming of Messiah.

2) The second bowl is poured out on the sea and it became blood (contaminated). This time all the living creatures of the sea are dead (not just one third).

3) The third bowl is poured on all rivers and springs of water so that no drinkable water remains.

4) The fourth bowl is poured out and the sun scorches men with fire. Perhaps the ozone layer fails amidst all the level of contamination and radiation in the atmosphere.

5) The fifth bowl immerses the beast kingdom (the one world empire) in total darkness. I perceive that since with the fourth bowl there is a sun that scorches

men with fire the sun now fries out the electrical grid
(**Rev. 16:10-11**)

6) The sixth bowl dries up the Euphrates River
which allows an army from the east (king of the East)
the ability to cross over to engage in the **battle of
Armageddon** along with other invading armies. This
last battle is referred to as "**the great day of God
Almighty**" (**Rev. 16:14**), probably because it brings
an end to the age of man.

On or around the battle of Armageddon the Lord
returns as we read in the verse that follows:

Rev. 16:15

*"Behold, I am coming as a thief. Blessed is he who watches, and
keeps his garments, lest he walks naked and they see his
shame."*

7 the seventh bowl judgment: After the seventh
bowl judgment is poured out on the air a great voice
declares *"it is done"* which releases the greatest
earthquake in history. It must break the Richter scale
along with everything else since the force of this
quake collapses mountains and Islands.

This massive earthquake is the final event of the age
of man as the remaining chapters of Revelation are
instructional as follows:

Revelation 17 & 18: These are two very important
prophecy chapters that describe who or what
"**Babylon the Great**" is. This great entity is so
important to end time events that God dedicates two
full chapters to this topic. This will be covered in detail
in another chapter.

Rev. 19: Describes the Messiah's second coming, with Jesus returning with His heavenly army to put an end to Satan and his minions. It also describes the Marriage Supper of the Lamb.

Rev. 20: Describes the Judgment of the antichrist, false prophet, Satan, the demons, zombies (sorry, I couldn't help it!), and all those who took the mark of the beast.

Rev. Chapter 21 - Describes the new Heavens and new earth - our glorious new home through eternity!

In Chapter 22: The revelation of Jesus Christ culminates in His words:

"I, Jesus, have sent my angel to give you this testimony for the churches. I am the Root and the Offspring of David, and the bright Morning Star."

My brothers and sisters in the Lord, as you now know, many prophetic signs are converging in 2015, making it quite possible that 2015 may be the harbinger year, warning that the apocalypse is imminent. So I believe that this book is one of the most important publications that I have ever penned.

Among the many crucial end time prophecies and topics that you will discover in Apocalypse Countdown - 2015 - 2021 are:

- Discover all of the key prophecies from all of the great ancient prophets; the key signs of the time of the end

- 2015 - the Harbinger Year
- Where is America in Bible Prophecy?
- The rise of America
- The coming fall of America
- Who is Babylon the Great - America?
- Why will Babylon the Great be Destroyed?
- Who will Destroy Babylon the great?
- How will Babylon the Great be Destroyed?
- Where will the antichrist establish his headquarters
- What nations will comprise the ten nation end time Empire
- Why is Jerusalem such a Burdensome Stone?
- What are the Consequences of Dividing up God's Land?
- The mystery of the Shemita blessings and curses.
- The Jubilee year connection
- The month of September and its link to financial and national disasters.
- Why there is more to 9/11 than most think?
- The coming seven trumpet judgments
- Who is the Beast of Revelation?
- Who is the 666 - the antichrist?
- Why will so many take the Mark of the Beast?
- The antichrist will come out of which Nation?
- Who are the Kings of North and South?
- Where is "Satan's throne" located?
- Left behind? What the prophecies reveal about the Rapture
- How to Survive the Coming Apocalypse
- Apocalypse Survival supplies and tips
- Emergency Supplies
- How to Prepare Emotionally and Mentally
- And more!

Again, I am not saying that 2015 is the year, but rather that from 2015 to 2021 we may indeed experience such great unrest and calamities throughout the world as discussed in this book, so that the controlling majority who are **void of the spirit of the living God** will force an unholy union in hopes for security. Tragically the security they secure will be a false security strait from hell!

This was a complimentary chapter from my new release:
"**Apocalypse Countdown - 2015 to 2021**"

Get Complimentary Access to: "Prophecy Alerts"

Dear Reader: Prophecies are being fulfilled so rapidly in these last days that I am offering my readers complimentary access to "*prophecy alerts*" so that you get "*Breaking Prophecy News*" as soon as it breaks…Just follow this link below and sign Up today…
http://robertritebooks.com/prophecy-alerts/

I appreciate your positive feedback

1) Visit and like our page at
https://www.facebook.com/RobertRiteBooks
2) Tweet "I recommend reading books @Robert Rite
3) Write a review on amazon.com or goodreads.com
4) Enjoy many articles at my blog:
http://robertritebooks.com

About Robert Rite

Robert Rite is the author of over 18 books including:

- "Apocalypse Countdown - 2015 to 2021"
- "Apocalypse Codes - Decoding the Prophecies in the Book of Daniel"
- "100 Proofs that the Bible is the Inspired Word of God and Scientifically Accurate"
- "Ancient Apocalypse Codes"
- "Awaken the Supernatural You!"
- "Aliens, Fallen Angels, Nephilim and the Supernatural"
- "Babylon the Great is Fallen, is Fallen! Who is "Mystery Babylon" of the End of Days?"
- "Blood Moons Rising"
- "Be healed!....How to Unlock the Supernatural Healing Power of God"
- "Bible Verses for Supernatural Blessings"
- End of Days
- "God, Mystery Religions, Cults, and the coming Global Religion"
- "Prophecies of the Apocalypse: Unlocking the End Time Prophetic Codes as Revealed by the Ancient Prophets"
- "Revelation Mysteries Decoded: Unlocking the Secrets of the coming Apocalypse"
- "Signs in the Heavens, Divine Secrets of the Zodiac & the Blood Moons of 2014!"
- "The New Age Movement vs. Christianity: and the Coming Global Religion"
- "Unlocking the Supernatural Power of Prayer"
- "128 Powerful Bible Verses that can Save Your Life!"

Robert is also the creator of over 135 articles on bible facts, and end-of-day mysteries and prophecies among other related topics. Visit Robert at RobertRiteBooks.com for sample chapters, press releases and related information.

Says Robert Rite:

"It is said that the truth at times is more stimulating than fiction. So *have the best of both worlds, and stimulate your mind and soul with subject matter - that really matters"*

<u>Robert Rite - Social Profiles</u>:
<u>Blog URLs:</u>
http://RobertRiteBooks.com

<u>Amazon Author Page</u>: http://www.amazon.com/-/e/B00GOGIBEG

Facebook Page:
https://www.facebook.com/robertritebooks
<u>Robert Rite at Twitter</u>
Twitter Handle: @robertrite
<u>You Tube Channel:</u>
https://www.youtube.com/channel/UCbED4FN2Pww-u-o1uO0qylQ
<u>Google Plus URL</u>:
https://plus.google.com/u/0/100112453810665259776/posts/p/pub
<u>LinkedIn:</u>
https://www.linkedin.com/profile/preview?locale=en_US&trk=prof-0-sb-preview-primary-button
<u>Pinterest:</u>
http://www.pinterest.com/frontierins/
<u>Stumble Upon:</u>
http://www.stumbleupon.com/stumbler/RobertRite

<u>Instagram</u>: https://instagram.com/robertrite/